aided and abetted by:
Margy Kinmonth
Jacqui Thomson
The Hon Marya Egerton Warburton
Shelagh Routh
Gloria McGowran
Countess Kristina von Merveldt

APICELLA

JONATHAN ROUTH'S

INITIAL
GOOD
LOO GUIDE

Where to 'Go' in London

BAN
YAN

First published in Great Britain in 1987
by Banyan Books, 363–365 Harrow
Road, London W9 3NA, U.K.

Exclusive Distribution in UK by
Book Sales Limited
8/9 Frith Street,
London, W1V 5TZ, UK.

ISBN No: 0.7119.1282.3
Order No: WC 10007

Cover printed by Creative Print and
Design, Harmondsworth, Middlesex.

Book printed by Anchor Brendon,
Colchester, Essex.

Designed by Sue Rawkins and David
McLeod at Campbell Rawkins, London.

Cover Design by Peter Hodkinson,
London.

Typeset by Chapterhouse,
The Cloisters, Formby

BANYAN Books and BEER
DAVIES
owe a very big thank you
to the following:
Sarah Crittendon
Ashley and Russell Leiman

INTRODUCTION

The entries in this Guide concern loos that I have encountered with assorted female companions during gentle toileteering ambles through the centre of London, just as I took some twenty years ago, and out of which emerged the first Good Loo Guide.

That was never a comprehensive Guide to all the loos of London – which would have been very long, very repetitive and very boring indeed. Nor is this present one. Its main purpose is just to remind the Toileteer that there are other loos than public loos to which he or she can have resource when he or she needs to.

Because these are grim days for Toileteers, much grimmer than twenty years ago. Not only are the majority of loos to-day conforming to a dull and featureless pattern, but public loos, those operated by City and Borough Councils, are rapidly disappearing – because they are difficult to staff, expensive to run, easy to vandalise, and liable to attract the wrong sort of customer anyway.

Actually, 'shrinking' might be a more accurate term to use than 'disappearing' because while some have been closed down and sold to the private sector and then – much to the detriment of Toileteers – re-opened as restaurants and billiard-halls, and others have been closed down and just left in their abandoned states while committees argue endlessly over what to do with them, yet others have been 'modernised' which has invariably meant, apart from the installation of very plain fittings, a reduction in the number of those fittings and the space taken up by the loo as a whole. In the last ten years Central London has lost, it is estimated, over 1250 public seats – altogether, counting cubicles, stalls and hand-basins, over 2800 toilet fittings. Which means that approximately every five minutes 2800 Toileteers – or just over 400,000 in each 12-hour day – who might once have patronized the great public loos of London are looking for Somewhere Else to Go. Nor are they going to be fobbed off with, let alone find adequate for their needs, 24 ridiculous 'Automatics' – those 10p-Automatic-Sliding-Door-Music-

Playing-Secret-Flushing-Seatless-Toilets which look like a contemporary version of Dr Who's normal form of transport – which Councils have erected at what they consider to be 24 strategic points around town. If they were used, even once every five minutes of a 12-hour day, they could give relief to a mere 3500 Toileteers.

So what is the poor Toileteer to do? Premises which have loos, and of which there are most around town, are pubs – the opening hours of which we are given to understand will run from 11 a.m. to 11 p.m. in 1988. This does not help the early-morning Toileteer however, nor are the conditions of the majority of pub loos conducive to happy toileteering at any hour of the day. With their cracked ceilings, peeling walls, and wet floors, with being cleaned but once a day, with being tucked away in converted coal cellars or the near-derelict back parts of pubs, they are normally filthy, disgusting small places. It is the brewers who are the villains of the piece. It is, after all, what is sold and consumed in their premises which generates so much of the Toileteer's basic need to visit loos. They should, therefore, act more responsibly concerning the state of these very essential departments of their establishments. Most restaurants – especially all new ones – provide clean aesthetically-pleasing loos. The pubs should be able to do so too.

And of course the other premises of which there is a reasonable abundance and which also have loos are hotels. But you can't very well go into some very grand hotel and just ask Which way is the loo, please, without dressing the part, without looking as though you're used to visiting its loo all the time. In fact, it's best not to ask at all where a hotel loo is, but to memorise from the entries in the Guide just exactly where they're positioned – first left inside the entrance, down a staircase and turn right through the swing doors – or whatever. Then, dressed in the style of the hotel, looking positively purposeful, you can walk boldly in and straight to your destination without any of the hotel staff guessing you might be only a visiting Toileteer. Good morning, you smile to any liveried flunkey you encounter – as though you've been seeing him every day for the past ten years – and of course at that moment you forget the Guide's instructions and, to the flunkey's amazement, walk straight into a broom cupboard.

So still, where is the Toileteer to go? I believe that the big Answer – as opposed to a lot of the little answers given in this Guide – could be the Privatisation of Loos. After all, British Rail is now planning the Privatisation of all station buffets and sandwich bars. Next on the list please, its loos. But they must stay loos. We do not want what has happened on Shepherds Bush Green, where it is the Toileteer who has been penalised by the Privatisation of the great loos there and the loos being turned into a billiard hall. At the same time, I submit, we need a man of vision (Richard Branson, are you listening?) to set up a chain of loos in every High Street, a branch in every street of consequence to the Toileteer. This way toileteering could be brought up out of the stygian depths where it normally has its being and become, at last, part of the very-nearly-21st Century we live in. The High Street loo could be a hairdressing establishment as well, a shop selling bathroom accessories, soaps, toilet rolls, contraceptives, cures for piles, and knickers. In fact as we are already reeling under the impact of Tie Shops and Sock Shops why not Knicker Shops as the name for them?

USING THE GUIDE

- Where no charge is given for the use of any facility mentioned in the Guide then the use of that facility is Free (which does not imply in some of the grander establishments that a Tip would not be welcome, or even expected, by the Attendant).
- The majority of loos which have a ground level venue are now fitted with special loos for the Disabled (which does not mean they are immediately available to the Disabled Toileteer, normally a bell has to be rung to summon an Attendant to open a door first)
- Opening Hours. Public loos – those operated by City and Borough Councils and British Rail – are very bad about advertising the hours their loos keep. They are also very suspicious of persons who ask attendants or phone other persons at head office to ask for information on the matter. Many open at 7.30 a.m. many close at 11 p.m., some like those on Waterloo Station even stay open all night. There is no general rule.

  Pub loos are open pub hours, store loos open store hours, and hotel loos, in theory, are open all the time. Your best bet if you're not sure when you might need one and whether anywhere will be open is to catch a long-distance train and rely on its loos.

  Failing that, remember that there are two Metropolitan Police Statutes that very few people seem to know about, and which, it is alleged, have never been Repealed. One is that a man in need may pee on the rear off-wheel of any conveyance in a public street. And a Lady under similar duress may command a Metropolitan Policeman to remove his cloak and hold it in such a way as to provide her cover from the public gaze.

***There are 3 gradings of loos in The Good
Loo Guide:***

★ ★ ★ Loos of real character and excellence.

★ ★ Very Good Loos Indeed.

★ Loos worth a Detour, not so much for their fittings
as for their ambience.

And there should be a 4th Grading, denoting Downright
Dirty and Disgusting Loos, but we will let the entries in the
Guide speak for themselves.

THE INITIAL GOOD LOO GUIDE AWARDS

The Good Loo Guide and Initial Textile Services are com-
bining to give out the first ever GOOD LOO GUIDE
AWARDS. The idea behind the awards is very simple – to
find and give recognition to loos that set the highest standards in terms of their character (fittings and design) and
excellence (cleanliness and service).

Only one set of Loos receives a ★ ★ ★ rating and these are:

**the under-the-pavement public loos of the Guildhall in
the City of London (p. 119). These loos receive the
Good Loo Guide ★ ★ ★ Award as the 'Best Loo
in London'.**

Five loos received ★ ★ awards – these are:

> **The Loo in The Portobello Hotel (p. 16)**
> **The Loos of Browns Hotel (p. 65)**
> **The Loos of The Wallace Collection (p. 86)**
> **The Euston Superloos (p. 90)**
> **The Loos of the National Portrait Gallery
> (p. 106)**

RECOMMENDATIONS

We are currently researching the full British Edition of The Good Loo Guide. We would welcome your suggestions for loos to be included whether they are in the form of recommendations or condemnations. Addresses and directions to their locations would obviously be useful.

Please send any correspondence to:
Banyan Books
363–365 Harrow Road
London W9 3NA

Any person using the name of this guide to obtain free facilities in a pay toilet is a fraud. Attendants, please inform the Police and us.

CONTENTS

THE LOOS OF PADDINGTON

The loos of Paddington Station

There's a number of quite pricy fittings in the **Gents** downstairs off Platform 1: 2 20p Pre-pasted Toothbrush Dispensers, 2 £1 Durex Featherlite machines; 1 50p Shower (Con-
tact Attendant); 20 insert-5p-coin-and-slide-knob cubicles –
within which the Toileteer is not totally invisible on account
of the frosted glass set in the doorways, and I have noted
some Toileteers of a shy or modest nature paste what paper is
available in their cubicle over this glass. I have also noted
some of the graffiti, mainly of political and anatomical
content, inscribed on the insides of the doors. Then there's a
Barber's Shop encased in glass which enables Toileteers to
watch Barbers and Barbers to watch Toileteers, and another
room with 8 very superior hand-basins and a bath in it, but
elsewhere there's a sign saying No Baths Any Longer.
Whether this is because the Attendant doesn't like naked
bathers wandering round his premises and getting the floors
all wet, or whether it's reserved just for the Barbers to bath in
after hours I don't know.

The **Ladies**, also attached to Platform 1, has 21 5p cubicles,
and 8 hand-basins (though on the day of my Inspector's visit,
no soap, no towels and the 2 electric hand-dryers not
functioning). My Inspector also points out that the printed
injunction not to ask the Attendant to look after your
luggage causes great hardship to lady Toileteers who may
want to keep an eye on their baggage and therefore have to
struggle into cubicles with it all.

The loos of The Great Western Hotel

approachable from the Station

Happier times for Lady Toileteers here. Turn to the right off
the main stairway to find a **Ladies** with 2 free cubicles, 3
hand-basins (with free hand lotion) and a rare hat-stand. In
the **Gents**, (turn left off the main stairway), accommodation
for 6 seated Toileteers, 8 standing, 3 abluting. And off these
spacious clean premises a large carpeted area – no furnishings
other than a full-length mirror – absolutely ideal for meeting

up with any West Country tailor willing to purchase a day-return to London and measure you for a new suit and subsequently to return and give you your fittings.

The loos of The Porchester Centre
North end of Queensway

I wasn't quite sure what this place was at all. Inside a rather grand pillared entrance was a lady issuing tickets from a box office and I asked her, 'did I need one to visit the loo?' 'No', she said, pointing to a door marked **Gents**. Inside the door, 134 numbered lockers and at the almost endless end of them, 2 cubicles. I entered one and shut its door, then realised that there was nothing, no single fitting or piece of furniture in the place. Nor any mark or blemish on the walls to indicate that any fitting had once existed here. So what was this cubicle for? Meditation? What a splendid idea. A sparse cubicle, a little chapel of your own, to which you could retire to spend 10, 15, 20 minutes away from the stress and bustle of the everyday world. Why didn't all public loos have them? I emerged from it, refreshed at least in spirit. Also here they had, apart from accommodation for meditationalists, accommodation for 3 Toileteers seated, 3 stalls and 3 hand-basins – and, I discovered as I went round the next corner, a communal shower for any number of naked men – well, there were three in it at that particular moment, vacancies for another ten I would have thought. (This place was getting increasingly weird). Just then 100 small boys wearing only swimming trunks burst through the room – and out of it, very quickly, on their way I quickly realised from the ensuing clamour, to plunge into an adjacent swimming-pool. So this was what the Porchester Centre was all about. Sadly I had to realise that my Meditation Rooms were in all probability Private Changing Rooms.

My Inspector of Ladies had a similar experience in her loo – except in the midst of near-naked ladies as opposed to naked men.

And if you want a rest from toileteering for a short while and join this lot using the pool you can hire everything you need from the lady in the box-office. You can even take just a normal bath or shower, but some of her charges are quite high, Towel Hire 70p, Soap Hire 20p, Comb hire 15p.

There are other loos at The Porchester Centre with Turkish Baths attached to them, but with an almost prohibitive entry fee of £7.50 (although you are allowed to stay in them for 3 hours for that sum).

apicella

The loos of Notting Hill Gate

Most Toileteers use those under the road at the entrance to the Underground. The blind accordionist who plays French street music at the door of the Gents is undoubtedly one of the place's attractions. Inside this **Gents**, one room with 6 hand-basins (2 Out of Order, and 1 rapidly becoming so), another room with 11 stalls, a curious green metal screen between each (anti-peeping device?), and a number of numbered Insert-10p-and-Slide-Knob cubicles. Behind the door of No 2 I found hand-written advertisements for Instant Circumcision, and much racist graffiti. And in another cubicle I noticed no toilet-roll holder nor evidence on the wall of there ever having been one attached to it, but an ample supply of brown cardboard on the floor which may not have been to every Toileteer's taste.

Perhaps, really, the only attraction of this place is the accordionist and his music.

In the **Ladies**, 6 10p cubicles, 6 hand-basins, long well-lit mirrors and much shining brass (but again, cardboard on the floor).

The loos of the Portobello Road

Way up the Road, where Goldbourne Road crosses it are loos under the road, just near to the Horse Meat shop and the Carnarvon Castle pub. In the old days the attendant at the **Gents** used to stand at the entrance-way and issue Toileteers with a meagre ration of paper, but he's gone now, and so have most of the other original fittings inside. There are stainless steel stalls and recessed Wallgate hand-basins. Only the dark wood doors of the 2 10p cubicles have survived the modernisers.

It's the same in the **Ladies**, except some of the original carpeting still seems to exist there.

● ● ● ● ●

Other subterranean loos are where Talbot Road intersects the Street Market, vaguely near the Tattoo Studio and West London Meat Market. In the **Gents**, 4 10p cubicles with steel doors, 5 stalls, 3 hand-basins and a 10p Weighing Machine. In the **Ladies**, much stainless steel, 6 10p cubicles, 2 hand-basins, light from glass tiles set in the pavement overhead, a unisex attendant lurking behind lace curtains, and a surprising number of lady Toileteers struggling to bring their supermarket trolleys down the steps – and up again.

● ● ● ● ● ●

★ ★ The best loo in this whole Portobello area is undoubtedly the unmarked one at the top of the stairs which lead down to the bar in *The Portobello Hotel* (22 Stanley Gardens). Small, just one lavatory and a tiny hand-basin, the whole room is done in a polished dark wood reminiscent of a previous more elegant age. If only public loos could look like this. . . .

The loos of Shepherd's Bush Green

I was never a regular at these loos on Shepherd's Bush Green, but every so often I would stop by to visit them and admire their large old-fashioned fittings. So imagine my surprise, when visiting them this year on behalf of this Guide to discover that they are no longer loos. An awning over one of the old ironwork staircases that leads under the Green

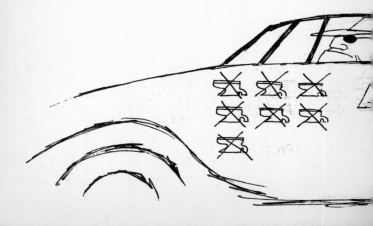

now proclaims that this is The Green Private Snooker and Social Club. I think to convert a large public loo into a premise which now contains 5 billiard tables (3 in the old Gents, 2 in the old Ladies), a bar and a set of small modern Members Only loos is a rather wonderful and very bold move. So that once, where all you heard was the flushing of cisterns, now all you hear is the clicking of balls. I wish the Middle Eastern owners all success in their enterprise. However, where does this leave the poor Toileteer?

There are two of the new automatic 10p loos, one on each corner at the bottom of the green, but these are not to be recommended unless the situation is desperate. The nearest alternative I can recommend are **the loos of The Kensington Hilton**, 179 Holland Park Avenue, at the bottom of Holland Park Avenue. In the **Gents** off the very bustling foyer, accommodation for 4 seated Toileteers (very smart louvred doors to the cubicles and 2 rolls of paper inside each), 6 standing Toileteers, and 4 abluting, and a Shoeshyne machine. Despite the premise's smartness it is really unbearably hot. In the **Ladies**, 4 smart cubicles, 4 well-stocked hand-basins and also a Shoeshyne machine – the only Ladies in town, I think, which can boast of such. Perhaps it's the air hostesses who make up such a large part of the place's clientele who demanded it. Also very hot and stuffy in there.

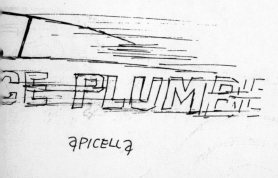

APICELLA

THE LOOS OF HYDE PARK AND KENSINGTON GARDENS

The multi-lingual loos of Hyde Park Corner

In the premises sign-posted and reserved for **Men, Messieurs, Herren** and **Signori** down the stairs at Pedestrian Subway Exit 3, 7 cubicles with glazed-glass doors (which has been no deterrent to the anatomical – but always English-language – graffiti-writers), 16 stalls, 4 hand-basins, and a roped-off overflow area containing a further 20 or so stalls and another 20 or so basins. Everything, except the graffiti, surprisingly clean. And in the **Ladies**, 4 hand-basins, 25 cubicles and various injunctions discouraging Loiterers. Also surprisingly clean – and, this being one of the Westminster chain, free. Open 7.30 a.m. to 11.00 p.m.

The loos of Marble Arch

Near to the monument which is Marble Arch you will see some high-jetting fountains. The loos of Marble Arch are below them. Virtually all underground passages in this part of London, mile after mile of them, from Park Lane, from Oxford Street, from the Bayswater road, from all over Hyde Park, from the Underground Car Park end up at them – there are altogether 14 entrances to the tunnels which will bring you out on the great below-ground-level sky-covered and tree-surrounded piazza which is the ante-room of the loos. It is vast this piazza, one of the most hidden large sites of the capital, a separate world from the rest of London, and yet on the day of our visit virtually empty. Perhaps Sunday afternoons, when Speakers Corner operates above, is the big day for Toileteers here, or when a Coronation processes by. Anyway, in the **Gents**, 12 cubicles, (enough graffiti on the backs of their doors to fill 2 vols, and most of it of the anatomical variety which would get the publisher immediately prosecuted if not required to leave the country), 5 new hand-basins, about 120 good old-fashioned stalls, and a 10p weighing machine. In the **Ladies**, 23 cubicles, 5 hand-basins, 1 6p washroom and a great library of cautionary notices prohibiting female toileteers from Loitering, warning them to Beware of Pickpockets, advising them where to get the latest information on V.D., cautioning them that the Police will be called immediately if they start Drinking, Drug-taking, or letting Any Dog Foul the Premises. (There's no exciting reading like this in the Gents at all).

The loos of Hyde Park Gate

A really fabulous array of flowers around these purpose-built free public loos in the Summer months – lilac, tulips, roses, exactly complimenting the red brick and shining chrome doors and railings of the place. In the **Gents**, 9 cubicles with brilliant orange painted doors, 4 stalls and 8 centre hand-basins. In the **Ladies**, 9 cubicles with brilliant yellow painted doors, and 3 clean – but plugless and soapless – inset hand-basins. Skate boarders prohibited in both premises.

Other loos of Hyde Park

At convenient intervals throughout the Park there are maps displayed which show the whereabouts of all the loos in the Park. One of the hardest to find – and not clearly marked on the map at all – is that situated between the Albert Memorial and the Serpentine Gallery. It is absolutely surrounded by bushes and has only the tiniest of signs saying Ladies and Gentlemen to denote that if you do penetrate these bushes you will encounter loos – clean and very recently built. In fact I'm wondering whether the Park Authorities know that they exist there at all – or could there be some eccentric philanthropist (because they're free) who's had them erected there because that's just the point where he and his family on their walks through the Park always get taken short.

There are others attached to the Serpentine Buffet, all with brilliant orange wall-panels. The **Gents** (1 cubicle, 3 stalls, 3 hand-basins) must rank as one of London's few triangular loos. The **Ladies**, at the time of our visit, with a foreign-looking lady in one cubicle, its door wide open, banging away on a typewriter. Well, it's not listed as a prohibitive activity in the Park Bye-laws (like playing musical instruments) and maybe in her country of origin all writers produce their best works by getting away to the peace and quiet of the loo.

Other loos at the restaurant the other end of the Serpentine; near the Police Station in the middle of that end of the park; near the Dogs Cemetery, opposite Lancaster Gate Underground; off the Bayswater Road at the bottom of Queensway; in the Children's Playground at the North West or Notting Hill Gate end of the Park (for children); at the Orangery near to there and to Kensington Palace; and also at Hyde Park Gate almost opposite the top of Gloucester Road. That leaves only the grandest Loos in Hyde Park and Kensington Gardens...

The loos of Kensington Palace

These are situated at the entrance to the State Apartments. In the **Gents**, 3 basins, 3 stalls, 3 cubicles. In the **Ladies**, 3 basins and 4 cubicles. Facilities for the Disabled in both.

Queen Victoria was born in the room over the Gents in 1819. She would have visited the room as its function in those days was the hanging of riding habits. But there is no evidence of there having been a souvenir and book shop at its door then.

Queen Anne actually died in these Gents in 1694, but the only Gent who seems to have had anything to do with them was King George II. He died in them in 1714.

Season tickets, valid for a year from date of issue, give admission to these and other loos looked after by the Department of the Environment. That is if you are also interested in looking round whatever building or monument is attached to the loos. Use of the loos themselves is free and does not necessitate producing any ticket.

THE LOOS OF KENSINGTON HIGH STREET

The Loos of The Royal Garden Hotel
Kensington High Street

Turn right inside the Hotel entrance and then right again by the Garden Restaurant. In the **Gents**, 2 cubicles, 5 stalls, 4 handbasins, 2 good hooks PLUS – and such largesse in loos has become increasingly rare to find – a tin of Andrews Liver Salts with wine glasses in which to dispense and mix it, an after-shave lotion, and a bottle of Listerine mouthwash. Also, in the ante-room, a small table with a phone on it.

In the **Ladies**, pink wall tiles and white marble flooring, elegant mahogany doors to the 4 cubicles, 4 marble encased hand-basins with gold-plated taps, much useful mirroring, much useful lighting, and a good upholstered chair to collapse in.

The loos of Kensington Market
Kensington High Street

They're beyond the milk-churn-furnished café at the back of the market. The door marked **Gents** leads into a room about three foot square without any fittings or furnishings whatsoever which had me a little baffled, but then one of its walls – which was what a flush door was masquerading as that day – swung open and a satisfied Toileteer emerged. The general state of this other room I found distinctly displeasing, so I left. In the next-door **Ladies**, 3 cubicles and one unconnected lavatory basin, and 2 disgusting basins, one falling off the wall, but plenty of soap. These premises, like the Market itself, are especially patronised by Punk Toileteers.

The loos of Kensington Town Hall
Hornton Street

The entrances to these loos are decorated with rather worrying placards – failing that, slightly puzzling placards (because I would have thought there could be no doubt about the lady's femininity) announcing – or warning you, that 'The attendant may be of either sex'.

In the **Gents** part of her domain, 6 'Insert 10p' cubicles (1

Free for the disabled) with king-size rolls of paper to compensate for the wretched little toilet seats; room for 11 full-size and 1 Dwarf Toileteer, and 12 hand-basins sharing 3 very small used pieces of soap. Paper towel dispenser for which I understand impecunious novelists who spend their days in the reading room of the public library upstairs are very grateful, alternatively Linen Towels which may be hired from the Attendant – if you ring for her – for 23p. For a few wipes of the hands it does seem a little excessive. For that sum, after all, I could have weighed both myself and a friend on the 10p machine in the room and still had 3p change. (Still, what can one do with 3p these days?). And anyway, probably the revenue from the hire of linen towels in this establishment is a fairly vital factor for Kensington Council in not adding another 23p to the rates.

In the **Ladies**, 10 cubicles at 10p (and a Disabled one Free), and 12 very clean hand-basins (sharing 4 little used pieces of soap), also 10p weighing machine and free drinking fountain.

My Inspector was particularly impressed by the vigour with which the chrome taps on the basins, and the brass bolts on the cubicle doors had been polished.

The loos of Marks & Spencers
99 Kensington High Street

Obviously a very continent type of customer here as there are no loos available to the public. One assistant recommended a visit to the Loos of the House of Fraser down the road.

The loos of The House of Fraser
63 Kensington High Street

The trouble, if you're in a hurry, is that you have to travel up two moving staircases to reach them – on the 2nd floor, turn left through Babywear toward the Restaurant. In the **Gents**, 4 Free cubicles, room for 3 standing Toileteers, and 3 hand-basins. Rather more of everything in the **Ladies**, plus, according to my Inspector's notes, 'songs and purchasing offers'. Come to think of it, there was an orchestra playing in the Gents . . .

The loos of C & A
160 Kensington High Street
None here either. They recommend you to those of BHS
(British Home Stores).

The loos of BHS
99-105 Kensington High Street
No moving staircases here, all the way up to the second floor
by your own efforts – and they're clearly marked 'Customers
Toilets'. Good, dull, purpose-designed hygenic rooms
making purposeful use of stainless steel. There's 1 stall for a
Dwarf amongst the 7 in the Gents, and a slightly time-
consuming device in all the cubicles which prevents you from
tearing off more than one piece of paper at a time.

The loos of Kensington High Street
Underground Station
Non-existent. Go out into the road, advised the ticket collec-
tor, or to McDonald's across the Street.

McDonald's fast loos
108 Kensington High Street
Downstairs. The extraordinary recessed hand-basins are to
allow more room for persons queueing for the cubicles – each

one of which (4 in the **Ladies**, 1 in the **Gents**) has 2 rolls of paper – both under lock and key. This doesn't prevent a criminal Toileteer from taking all the paper but he (or she) will have to re-roll it themselves.

The loos of 99 Kensington High Street

The entrance to the loos of this rather hidden Exhibition Centre is in the side-street between the House of Fraser and Marks and Sparks. Take the lift to the 3rd floor, which seems to be called the Ladbroke Suite, ignore anyone who has the impertinence to ask you what you're doing, and turn left through the first doors you see, just before other doors which lead into whatever Exhibition is going on. In the **Gents**, accommodation (in shocking red and orange cubicles) for 6 Toileteers seated, 4 standing and 6 abluting. In the **Ladies**, grey carpetting, lime green and navy decor elsewhere, 3 cubicles (choice of papers), 4 hand-basins with Monobloc Mixer taps (there are probably lady Toileteers who will use only basins with these), large mirrors and a facility for the Disabled.

My Inspector of Ladies insists that these are Designer Loos. My own thought about them is that if there's something interesting going on in the Ladbroke Suite, like a Wine or Luxury Foods Exhibition for the trade only, you can probably get into it by striking up a relationship in the loo with an Exhibitionist Toileteer and go back into the place arm in arm with him.

The loos of The Commonwealth Institute

Kensington High Street

Plenty here, basement and 2nd floor, the **Gents** dull, hygenic. My Inspector in the basement **Ladies** praises the rare full-length mirror, but has reservations about the over-flow pipes from the cisterns in the cubicles, the possibility of damaging yourself should you lean back on them, or getting very wet indeed, even drowning should they suddenly start to overflow. A rare extra in the Institute's bookshop – packets of beautiful loose-leaf multi-coloured Indian loo paper. A great pity to put it to any other use than decorating walls or writing to ones loved ones – and who can say that about any English paper?

● ● ● ● ● ●

Just before you get to the entrance from the High Street to the Institute is the entrance to Holland Park and here is something very rare indeed. 'DOG LAVATORY' reads a large sign over a six by six foot sandpit. 'Please encourage your dog to use this facility before proceeding further in the park.' Beside it there was a child crying because his mother or nanny wouldn't let him stop to play in it.

● ● ● ● ● ●

The loos of Leighton House Art Gallery
12 Holland Park Road
The sound of falling water in the fountain of the Arab Room drives you to them even if that was not your original intention when you came to Leighton House. There are The Guest ones, downstairs, clean and unremarkable, but not nearly as used as other Loos in the High Street. Lord Leighton's personal loo I suspect, is half way up the main staircase and push back a particular section of the black-coated pannelling. Contributions toward the upkeep of these rare loos is very acceptable in a glass case nominated for the purpose near the entrance in the lobby.

The loos of Holland Park
In converted stables adjoining the delightful Orangery in the middle of the Park, and just near to the Childrens Sand Pit are these filthy loos. In the **Gents** 2 dirty cubicles, an L-shaped row of smelly stalls, a 10p weighing machine in lieu of any hand-basin. And yet, outside, roses all around, creepers up the walls, peacocks wandering by – it's quite amazing by contrast. And in the **Ladies** in the same building, you think you're about to walk into some pleasant rustic cottage and all you find inside is 2 cubicles (pieces of string to pull instead of any proper chains) and no basin.

On the other side of the pathway where these sorry loos are situated a Portaloo, complete with hand-basin has been installed. It is an infinitely preferable place to visit.

★ Also infinitely preferable are the loos of London's most charmingly situated restaurant, **The Belvedere**, adjoining the other side of the Orangery. Unfortunately they do rather expect you to eat there, or at least sample their incredible collection of 92 Malt Whiskies before they let you into their small smart loos (off the staircase and open only 12.00 to 2.30 p.m. and 6.30 to 10.30 p.m.).

THE LOOS OF CHELSEA

The loos of San Lorenzo
22 Beauchamp Place
The loos of this most famous of all Italian restaurants in
London were replumbed in 1986 and now more than ever
live up to the reputation they had acquired before then. The
secret of their charm, and why so may Toileteers in this area
flock to them, is the flowers selected at Covent Garden early
each morning by Mara, wife of the proprietor Lorenzo Berni.
Mara spends an inordinate length of time arranging them
around the basins, as well as personally checking on the
cleanliness of each fitting in the premises, (**Gents**, 2 cubicles,
1 stall, 2 hand-basins; **Ladies**, 2 cubicles, 2 very pretty hand-
basins). Americans come from far and wide, and probably
from America too, to marvel at the soft waters and subtle
soaps served in these little floral temples – so always best to
book (584-1074) and state which sitting you'd prefer.

The loos of Sloane Square
The usual ridiculous Kensington and Chelsea restrictions
apply to these Council loos, so be prepared. The Attendant
does not give change, No Shaving or Loitering, No Dogs,
and there's one printed Bye-Law which reads exactly like
Groucho Marx talks in his 'Party-of-the-first-part' piece in
'A Night at the Opera'. 'A-person-of-the-male-sex-shall-not-
enter - or - use - any - convenience - set - aside - for - the - use - of -
persons-of-the-female-sex-and-a-person-of-the-female-sex-
shall-not-enter-or-use-any-convenience-set-aside-for-the-use-
of - persons - of - the - male - sex. . .' But the attendant in the
Gents is a nice fellow, a real professional who campaigned
successfully some little while ago for the provision of litter
baskets in the Square as otherwise 'everybody used to kick
their litter down my steps and what they didn't kick the wind
blew'.

Downstairs in his **Gents**, 5 10p cubicles, 9 stalls, 2 free
hand-basins.

Downstairs in the normally very clean **Ladies**, 6 10p
cubicles, 4 free hand-basins.

The loos of The Royal Court Tavern
Sloane Square

In the **Gents**, towards the back of the establishment, 2 stalls, 2 hand-basins, 1 free cubicle. Pretty grim, but not if you need to save 10p. My Inspector of **Ladies** at first blanched at visiting her allotted territory, but subsequently found them to be quite spotless. Perhaps it's only male Toileteers who make such a mess of pub loos.

The loos of Peter Jones
Sloane Square

On the plan of the store there are shown loos for **Ladies** on the 2nd, 3rd and 4th floors. Our Inspector cleverly managed not to discover the first two, but was lucky on the 4th floor and found 3 free cubicles, 4 hand-basins and a dressing table. 'Left off lift through first door on left,' read her directions, 'straight down four steps' – if that helps.

The only **Gents** in the store is also on the 4th floor, just outside the Crockpot Coffee Shop, 3 stalls, 2 free cubicles, 2 hand-basins and yards and yards of roller towel.

The loos of The General Trading Centre
144 Sloane Square (bottom of Sloane Street)

Ladies, left of the stairs ahead of the front door just by the prints of ducks or similar birds, 2 cubicles and 2 small hand-basins. **Gents**, turn right inside front door and it's a tiny little premises (1 cubicle, 1 hand-basin) in the middle of Wicker Furniture and Plastic Flowers.

The loos of Antiquarius Market
135–141 King's Road

At the back of the store by the cafe, nothing antiquated about these small free loos. *Very* preferable to some of the filthy pub loos in the neighbourhood.

The loos at the bottom of Sydney Street
off King's Road

These are a great favourite with taxi-drivers – one of whom first introduced me to them. I also have a report of a No 49 bus-driver who's a regular. For the rest it's a fairly dull crowd of Toileteers who patronise these clean dull little premises not for themselves alone, but as an alternative to the filthy conditions to be found in the majority of the loos of the pubs in the Kings Road.

One snag is that there's a 10p charge for use of the cubicles in both Ladies and Gents, another is the restriction on Shavers and Loiterers. Use of the hand-basins is free though.

The loos of The National Army Museum
Royal Hospital Road

Conveniently situated for Cheyne Walk, visits to Thomas Carlyle's House and the Chelsea Flower Show when in season, these loos must rank as possibly the plainest in all London – which is not any complaint regarding their function, they are simply very, very plain. Down two flights of stairs, take your bearings from the great portrait of Lt. General Rowland Hill wearing the Order of the Bath, and in the **Gents** 4 cubicles, a row of stalls and 3 hand-basins; in the **Ladies**, 4 cubicles, 4 hand-basins, 2 chairs and a leather-topped desk.

PROBLEM PLUMBER

apicella

THE LOOS OF KNIGHTSBRIDGE

The loos of The Berkeley Hotel
   Wilton Place

The **Gents**, on the ground floor, straight ahead of the front door – very smart indeed, the attendant busy polishing the mirrors as I entered which labour he dropped immediately to top up a hand basin with hot water for my prospective use. I forget how many hand basins there were, 10 stalls though and each with a handsomely framed Spy cartoon at eye level over it; and 4 cubicles, at least two of which also had bidets in them beside the lavatory basin. These are quite unique in all of the Gents of London, as well as being totally baffling to me. I should be interested to hear from any Toileteers who make a regular point of using them and for what. Also in the establishment, many ashtrays and a modest saucer for tips.

The bidet-less **Ladies** nearby is also very smart with an attendant waiting with cotton towels and fresh soaps at the basins – gold plated taps incidentally.

There is a legend that the Queen has patronised these loos but I suspect it is more likely it was a member of the party she was lunching with in the Restaurant. Certainly no plaque up to commemorate the event.

The loos of the Hyde Park Hotel
   66 Knightsbridge

Up the stairs inside the entrance and clearly marked. **Ladies** – well, here are my Inspector's notes: '5 wash-basins, gold taps, soap and Att, hand towels or tissues, large mirrors, carpets, bright spacious flowers and chairs'. I'm sure there were some cubicles as well. **Gents**, up a further flight of stairs – to the left, I think – 4 cubicles, 6 stalls – my notes don't say how many hand-basins, but they do state that beside them were some Useful Extras – a mouthwash, a hairspray and a bottle of Malvern Spring Water with glasses.

The loos of Harvey Nichols
   Knightsbridge

The star is the **Ladies** on the 3rd floor. A huge vaulted room with 7 cubicles, 7 hand-basins, masses of marble and mirroring, 2 chairs and a telephone. The **Gents** on the 3rd floor is relegated to an outside landing through Bedding – 1 cubicle, 3 stalls, 2 hand-basins.

Also little, rather scruffy loos for both sexes in the basement cafe.

The loos of The Basil Street Hotel ★
Basil Street

The **Gents**, up the main stairs and turn left up a further old-fashioned, carpeted country-house staircase just before the Parrot Club; 2 cubicles, 3 old-fashioned marble and tile hand-basins, and a desk, one drawer of which contained 400 pieces of used soap.

The **Ladies**, *down* the staircase just before the Parrot Club, to a pleasant country-house type room with 3 cubicles, 2 hand-basins, 1 Attendant, tall mirrors, and a rare (these days) assortment of brushes, cotton wools, creams and colognes. A desk in the alcove just outside the room with a telephone.

The loos of Harrods
Knightsbridge

There are mysteries here I cannot fathom. The oldest loos in Harrods are the underground **Gents** you approach down the staircase next to Mens Tailoring (entrance at the back of the building). Down these stairs you find them clearly arrowed, adjacent to the Mens Hairdressing establishment and the curious olde-worlde Green Man Pub. But on the actual loo doors you must go through the sign saying, boldly, Emergency Exit. The large room it gives into is a mixture of fourteen different styles of architecture and decoration, as though 14 different interior decorators worked on it at the same time – Art Deco decorators, school of Klimt decorators, Black chrome and glass door decorators, marble floor and wall decorators. And they each got their way – for some of the room. Basically there are 4 cubicles, 5 stalls and 5 marble-set basins in the inner area; and 2 telephone alcoves and 2 chrome and leather chairs for those who would have their shoes polished in the entry area. There is no set charge for this latter indulgence but the attendant who preened my footwear said that most persons give him £1 or £2.

There's the noise of machinery reverberating through the room, rather like the distant roar of a ship's engine room and this, mingling with the flushing of the loos, and the persons dressed as cooks and ships officers who from time to time rush through the room as though practising lifeboat drill definitely put you in mind of being at sea on board something like the old Queen Mary. Who are these persons? Why is the door marked Emergency Exit? Why are there trapdoors set into the floors of the cubicles? And why is there this sign outside which reads 'Customers are requested to take care of all personal belongings especially handbags'. It does suggest a rather special sort of customer surely, and the sign continues, 'customers are reminded of the cloakroom facilities available at the Parcels Office on the 4th floor'.

I went up to this Parcels Office on the 4th floor, but they disclaimed any knowledge of Gentlemens Loos in their vicinity and suggested I try the Georgian Restaurant elsewhere on this same floor. Several miles and many enquiries later I found these loos, a fine padded door at their entrance and against which you can bang your head to be vent of all frustrations acquired during your search. A fine set of loos inside, accommodations for 3 shopping Toileteers seated, seven standing (at rather pretty blue porcelain stalls), and 6 washing their hands of the whole shopping affair spree. They look absolutely new, which is a tribute to Herman Freire, one of the world's great lavatory attendants who has been with them since they first opened in 1975, a man proud of his job and his premises, who has old-fashioned standards of cleanliness – and also a mysterious large bottle of Green Stuff on the table in the middle of the room the function of which I completely forgot to ask him.

So we come to the **Ladies** loos. There are Ladies loos littered all over Harrods – all together, if my Inspectors' arithmetic is correct, 86 Cubicles and 82 hand-basins. That is a lot. Their main concentration seems to be around Lingerie on the 1st floor. In the one, 14 cubicles, 12 hand-basins, centre dressing tables and mirrors at which Toileteers try on bits of clothing and try out make-up and fragrances, while an attendant is continuously at work wiping, washing and spraying the room around them. In the other, 12 hand-basins, and 12 cubicles (in some of which one of my Inspectors claims to have found, beside the lavatory basins, mystery urinals. When she asked the attendant for what reason they were there the attendant said she'd often wondered about them herself, whether they were wash-basins or what, but that anything odd in these loos was because they'd once been the Gents loos and the conversion had been done in a hurry). There quite obviously used to be a shower room in this loo too, in disuse now except for the storage of brooms. While in the Ladies on the 2nd floor, between Beds and Books, apart from the normal 12 cubicles and 12 hand-basins there's a working cold shower, but no record, according to the attendant, of any Toileteer ever having asked to use it. Other Ladies, without showers, on the 4th floor between Prints and Lending Library. And the grandest Ladies of all, according to one Inspector, by the Trafalgar Bar – near to Books – with rouched curtains – whatever they may be – stippled walls, 5 blue, white, mahogany and brass cubicles, 6 really fabulous hand-basins with gold taps resting on rococo wood pedestals, and 2 assistants 'willing to do anything you ask them' – Oh, the lucky Lady Toileteers of Harrods.

The loos of Knightsbridge Crown Court
1 Hans Crescent, behind Harrods
You never know who you might be toileteering alongside here. Normally you get a very good class of Toileteer – despite the fact that he's probably being questioned about a several-million pound fraud or tax evasion – but he's still probably a sound Toileteer. Loos on every floor, the only things odd

about them being that the police give you a polite search before you enter, and the lids of the cisterns are padlocked on to the cisterns. So that you can't conceal the contents of your pockets? To avoid last-minute incriminating evidence being hidden? Or just because there's a band of thieving barristers who practice in the building and think it's 'Very Funny' to make off with cistern lids?

The loos of South Kensington Underground Station

There are no loos at the station. The ticket inspector we turned to for advice suggested we took a train to Earls Court Station where he suspected they still had such facilities (q.v.). A poster beside him appealed to us to travel up the M1 to Sheffield on a Rapide bus which it claimed had a toilet on board.

Instead, we looked outside the station and saw **The Norfolk Hotel**, (Harrington Road). Cheerful men in top hats directed us to perfectly adequate loos on the ground floor there. In the **Gents**, 2 of everything, and telephone and cigarette machine in the passage outside. In the **Ladies**, also 2 of eveything Ladies need, plus sultry music.

Not far away, in Glendower Place, we then visited **the loos of the Moti Mahal Tandoori Restaurant**, Woodfall Court, 2 Smith Street. I think they were a little surprised we didn't want to sit down and enjoy a dish of bindi bhaji, but I muttered something about looking for a lost friend in the loo, and they seemed quite happy. Downstairs it is, just off the kitchen, a little premises, sufficient enough; and outside it, a coat rack, the contents of which suggests the place is patronised by a very good – if forgetful – class of Toileteer; all black ties, black waistcoats and black jackets left hanging there.

Les cabines de l'institut Francais (The loos of the French Institute)

17/29 Queensberry Place

Downstairs, in the **Hommes**, accomodations, in blue, for 2 Toileteers seated, 6 standing, and 2 abluting. For **Femmes**, also in blue, 5 cubicles, and 2 cuvettes (or hand-basins). Nothing mysteriously different about these places except that most of the Toileteers are speaking French ('Au secours! Je suis enferme!' means 'Help, I am locked in the loo', but I didn't know that until I looked the words up in a dictionary and by then it was probably too late to do anything about it). There was also a room for a third category of Toileteer, Professors – that is if *Refectoire des Professeurs* means Loo for Professors. There might have been something mysteriously different in it but as it was locked I couldn't find out.

★ *The loos of The Science Museum*

In this Museum, in the Domestic Appliance Galleries downstairs, is the finest surviving Victorian Bathroom in London. The actual loo, or Water Closet (W. C.), is a New Humber by McDowell Stevens & Co., circa 1880, a typical lavatory installation of the period with elaborately painted pedestal, mahogany seat and cover and an overhead siphon tank with ball valve. It was presented to the Museum by the Executors of Brigadier W. Clark, deceased (Old W. C. I dare say they used to call him).

The wash-basin alongside is marble with a mahogany case and remarkable pull-up taps and it was once the property of a Duke of Westminster.

The actual bath, a magnificent structure, has 7 taps arranged vertically on the side of the shower wall – to operate a spray, a douche, the shower, a plunge, hot and cold water and the waste.

The sad thing about it all is that the public can only *look* at this bathroom behind plate glass windows. But its's nice to think that, on very special occasions, like for instance, the anniversary of the Prince Consort's birthday, the Trustees of the Museum actually get around to using it as it should be used.

There are actual usable loos all over the building, but the easiest to find are those on the Ground Floor. The **Gents** are situated between Internal Combustion Engines and Exploration of Space (with a sign on one cubicle door reading 'Permanently Out of Order'), the **Ladies** a little further down the gallery beside the White Steam Car exhibit.

A sign on a large glass box in the entry hall of the building explains that while entry to the Loos of the Science Museum is free they do cost £1 a second to run and some Toileteers might care to make a donation toward their upkeep i. e. please spare a coin for the glass box. And as a whole new wing of the building, devoted entirely to loos, is now under construction, I suspect such donations will be doubly welcome. **Note**: these loos and all other Museum loos cannot be recommended to early-morning Toileteers as they do not open until 10.00 a.m.

Next door to the Science Museum are the ***loos of the Geological Museum*** where you are asked to pay a £1 entry fee to the building before you can use them, so as a canny Toileteer I am dismissing these.

It's even more exorbitant to use the ***loos of the Natural History Museum*** – a £2 entry fee. But they're free on Mondays to Fridays from 4.30 p.m. to 6.00 p.m., and Saturdays and Sundays and Bank Holidays from 5.00 p.m. to 6.00 p.m. – if you can hold out that long.

The loos of The Victoria and Albert Museum

These had me totally flummoxed. I studied the plan of the building displayed every now and then on the walls, full of little symbols promising the existence of Ladies and Gents. I walked I should say down four miles of not uninterestingly ornamented galleries, but loos I just could not find. Then a workfellow I encountered told me they'd all been ripped out – which I don't think Victoria or Albert, if they'd have been in a hurry, would have been very pleased about. I suppose this is just further testimony to what some papers have described as the 'disastrous 13-year reign' of the Museum's Director Sir Roy Strong, unless it is that the Government is just refusing to provide enough funds for the upkeep of the loos here. Whatever, what was once one of the richest collections of loos in Western Europe is now reduced to a few piles of rubble, damning proof of the shameless way Britain treats its artistic heritage.

It was looking for some alternative loos that I wandered out into Exhibition Road and came across almost next door, and totally unexpectedly. . .

The loos of The Church of Jesus Christ of Latter-Day Saints

On the ground floor just past the Information Desk lie the **Gents** (3 cubicles, 3 stalls, 3 hand-basins). But I never discovered where the Ladies laid, on account that the Inspector of Ladies I had with me on my entry to the building, and who then departed from me on her quest, never re-appeared. Nor have I heard from her since. Surely – surely – she couldn't be the original of the Lady still Locked in the Lavatory? This was *weeks* ago.

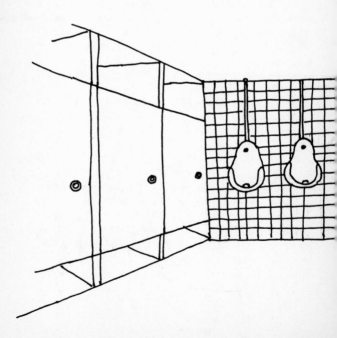

The loos of The Royal Albert Hall

The only way I could find to visit a loo here without also attending a Concert was to join a £1 mini-tour of the place. As a good Toileteer I wouldn't have minded so much if it had been a mini-tour of the Loos of the Albert Hall – in fact, to begin with, I thought it might be, as we were told we would see what they referred to as the Queen's Box, and what they also called 'other visual displays' – but it was far from being all loos. Though at one point when we came across a very life-like life-size wax model of Prince Albert talking to us I couldn't be absolutely sure on what he was sitting behind his desk. And when the mini-tour eventually went past the Gents on the ground floor near Gate No 8 and the tour leader ignored it altogether I was so disgusted that I asked to be excused. Inside this **Gents** were 3 cubicles, 3 hand-basins and 14 stalls being contantly flushed by giant Twyford

cisterns which made such an avalanche of noise that it drowned even the strains of the orchestra rehearsing on the stage of the Hall, and which the acoustics of the loo made so available to visiting Toileteers.

It was only afterwards that I started wondering whether the acoustics of the whole Hall made it likely that those seated in the auditorium also heard the flushings of the giant Twyfords during concerts. Alright if Handel's Water Music was on the menu but a little disconcerting otherwise.

There are adequate – and quieter – loos for **Ladies** in the Hall, and the mini-tours are from June to October only.

The loos of Gloucester Road Underground Station

There are no longer any loos at the station and when you ask the staff there for advice they recommend the loos of the Wimpy over the road. Well, perhaps that's where they may go, but personally, I'd choose the ***loos of the Bombay Brasserie*** round the corner. The Brasserie shares its loos with Bailey's Hotel next door and you can, in fact, make a more inconspicuous visit to them by using the hotel entrance, walking straight ahead through 3 sets of swing doors and then turning right. In the **Gents**, accommodation for 3 Toileteers seated, 3 standing and 3 abluting. In the **Ladies**, 4 cubicles, 3 hand-basins, a lot of dripping noises and the smell of Indian cooking. These are not very special loos. Nor are the loos of the rather ostentatious and Arab-orientated **Gloucester Hotel**, 4 Harrington Gardens, just down the road. In the **Gents** on the 1st floor, paper all over the floor and running taps. The same in the **Ladies**, plus a rather mysterious smell (endlessly recycled air?) and something which hardly any other loo boasts (or perhaps feels it needs to have), a Fire Blanket. Well, the thought of a female Toileteer setting herself on fire, or even setting another Toileteer on fire, is not a very pleasant one, but at least this Hotel faces up to the possibility.

There are other loos in other hotels around here, but, all in all, Gloucester Road is a pretty desolate area for Advanced Toileteers.

The loos of Earl's Court Underground Station

Down a few steps from the station entrance and turn left, this is the shape of loos to come, very modern, compact, clean (very good considering that a few years ago these were two of the drabbest, dirtiest rooms in all England).

In the **Gents**, 3 10p cubicles, 4 stainless steel stalls, and 3 'Wallgate' hand-wash devices – these being small stainless steel basins recessed into the wall. You press one button to produce water (warmish), a second button to produce a dribble of soap, and a third for hot air – all the time keeping at any rate one hand in the recess referred to as the basin.

Similar devices in the **Ladies**.

THE LOOS OF BELGRAVIA AND PIMLICO

The loos of The Hyatt Carlton Tower
Cadogan Place

Very small clean loos on the ground floor (turn left through the entrance). Real flowers and proper towels in the **Ladies**, (3 cubicles, 3 hand-basins), the same in the **Gents** (similar accommodations) plus bottles of Evian water. In neither loo is it possible to hear the pianist who plays in the adjacent Chinoiserie Lounge, which is a pity. On the other hand, in the Chinoiserie Lounge you can't hear the flushing of the loos, which is perhaps all to the good.

The loos of the Belgravia Sheraton
20 Chesham Place

Down the narrow stairway to the left of the front door. Beautifully laundered towels in the **Ladies** (3 cubicles, 3 hand-basins) and paintings on the walls. But these cubicles, and the 2 in the **Gents** (2 hand-basins in there as well) are curiously small and narrow – which may be deliberate and aimed at attracting a thinner class of Toileteer, alternatively this may be some subtle form of discrimination against over-sized Toileteers.

The loos of Pimlico Green
(Which the observant Toileteer will note is not green at all, it's completely paved – I mean where Pimlico Road and Ebury Street intersect).

In the **Gents**, 5 free cubicles, room for 11 standing and 1 hand-basin – there used to be 2 as the fittings on the wall indicate but some greedy Toileteer made off with the other. In the **Ladies**, 5 free cubicles and 2 wash-basins.

Both loos, operated by Westminster Council, have been cleaned and managed for the last five years by a Mr Silver who may sometimes be in the Gents, other times – much to the consternation of casual visitors to the establishment – in the Ladies. Just before our visit, he told us, a female Toileteer had gone berserk in the place (that is, the Ladies, while he, Mr Silver, was ministering to his Gentlemen). He returned to the Ladies to find it knee-high in books the lady had emptied out of suitcases, 'Lovely stuff, nearly all poems'. So now Mr Silver is wondering whether to set up a Ladies Lending Library as well.

The loos of Buckingham Palace

It's no good stopping and saying 'Excuse me but I'm a Loyal Subject, would you direct me to the Gents', or, 'Can you tell me where the Ladies is, please'. You have to be *invited* to use these loos. Like, H. M. the Queen phones to say 'Please come and collect an OBE (or Dukedom) next Thursday at 3.30 p.m. if you're doing nothing else', or, she's sent you a post-card saying 'Do come to the super Garden Party I'm giving next Friday at 4.00 p.m'.

And we know, from The Beatles when they went to the Palace to collect their decorations and retired to the loos to have a little relaxing smoke, that there's nothing very incredible about these loos. They are not converted thrones with lift-up seats, nor do they have velvet seat covers you can make off with as a souvenir of your visit. And Garden Party-going Toileteers won't even get into the Palace because portable loos are erected under canvas in the garden for their needs.

Other Toileteers who might find themselves in the Queen's Gallery at Buckingham Palace (for which privilege they will have paid an entry fee of £1.10) will be told by one of the Queen's very splendidly costumed servants – all black, red, gold and white, that there are no loos available to them there and will be directed into Buckingham Palace Road outside the building, told to turn right there until the next traffic lights where they must make a left and follow signs saying TOILET until they find same. They won't, but at least they're given a free ticket of re-admission to the Gallery – I just hope that such treatment is not meted out to Visiting Heads of State and other dignitaries inside the Palace proper.

THE LOOS OF VICTORIA

The loos of Victoria Station

These were, at the time of going to press, unimaginably foul. The large **Ladies** upstairs below Platform 18 (next to left luggage) full of mostly large ladies, fighting, snarling, crying because they hadn't got the right change for the facility they wanted to use (10p for the use of lavatory and a hand basin, 70p for a bath or shower, 30p for a dressing room), or they felt others were usurping their place in the queue to get at the facilities or most probably because after all this delay they were missing train after train (which if they'd paused to think had free lavatories and hand basins and no queues on them anyway).

The **Gents** (but see also p. 51) alongside here is without doubt the most disgusting premises in town. A foul-smelling caravan containing minimal facilities for Toileteers seated, standing and abluting, its floor awash, and a large sign outside offering apologies for its conditon. But until the renovation of the station is complete this is what has to serve the 265,460 male toileteers who pass through Victoria every day. One needs an alternative in the neighbourhood, but where?

First of all there's the vast ***Grosvenor Hotel*** which seems to be part of Victoria Station and has one entrance off the same platform as the notorious Gents caravan (though, either for curious reasons of their own, or of security, the Management prefer you to use the entrance in Buckingham Palace Road). Make towards Edward's Bar and you will find a spacious if slightly untidy **Ladies** (5 cubicles, 5 wash-basins) and a perfecty adequate **Gents** (old-fashioned music for the swinging Toileteer piping out).

However, these premises are not of a size to accommodate all the teeming Toileteers of Victoria Station.

So, out into the streets around the Station, everywhere arrowed signs directing you to TOILETS. Follow them, as hundreds of others – presumably fellow-Toileteers – appear to be doing. And we all end up under the road outside the station at two totally closed premises. It's a shabby trick on the part of Westminster Council to keep up these signs and so give false hope to needy Toileteers. What is their plan for the premises, I wonder, now they have closed them? An underground Garden Centre? Railwaymens Night Club? Extension from the Channel Tunnel? We shall see.

We still need alternative loos to the station though.

Westminster Cathedral is nearby. The Loos of Westminster Cathedral? Inside they tell me, rather severely, that Cathedrals do *not* have plumbing and that most of their customers who have any need of plumbing patronise McDonald's across the way. Yes, there are free, small, clean adequate loos in the basement of McDonald's – no queues of clerics – but the premises are still too small to cope with the traffic volume of Toileteers that Victoria Station generates.

Victoria Coach Station is nearby, down Buckingham Palace Road, the other direction from the Cathedral.

The **Gents** is after your money. Five cubicles (insert 5p coin and Slide Knob), 5 free stalls, and 5 hand-basins (no charge for the soap for there is no soap), and an Annexe containing roughly the same amount of facilities again. Around the establishment the following attractions:

- coin-operated electric razor (insert 3x10p)
- machine dispensing pre-pasted disposable toothbrushes (insert 2x10p)
- machine dispensing Durex Featherlite (electronically tested) insert £1 coin for pack of 4
- trilingual electric shoeshine machine (insert 10p and see what happens)
- and then something which says Brut for Men 10p. *'Bitte knopf mehrmals durchdrucken'* it advises (Depress button fully several times). While you do this and hold one hand under it in anticipation of receiving some little pot of largesse, it squirts stuff at you, or rather, at whatever part of you happens to be nearest the squirt's nozzle – in my case, my left jacket shoulder. I think I've mastered the technique now for when I want it on my tie.

IN ⬇
10p

The **Ladies** at this establishment is not a very appetising sight. 28 5p cubicles, 12 hand-basins, 4 electric hand-driers, no dogs allowed, open 6.00 a.m. to midnight. My inspector was inclined to agree with Mrs Lambert the attendant for the last 12 years that there's nothing really bad about the place, it's a lot of the people who use it who are absolutely filthy.

The alternative of course if you seek privacy from such company is to book on to a Rapide bus and hide in the free loo in its rear.

Nearby to the Coach Station, out of the Semley Place exit, – though we're getting further away from Victoria Railway Station – are *the loos of the Ritz Snooker Club*. These are situated in one of the most exciting locations of any set of Loos in London, with 10 full-size billiard tables on one side of them and another 10 on the other side. Room for 3 standing, 3 seated and 2 abluting in the **Gents**. In the **Ladies**, 3 cubicles, 3 hand-basins, chairs and mirrors – (including one rare full-length). Very good clean free loos indeed.

Back to the other side of Victoria Station there are two alternative loos worth mentioning. **The loos of the Brasserie St Germain** (which is part of the Royal Westminster Thistle Hotel) in Buckingham Palace Road – don't worry, nothing curiously French about them. Just pleasantly decorated adequate loos for both Gents and Ladies.

Then *the loos of the Rubens Hotel* also in Buckingham Palace Road. Veer slightly left through the main entrance door, you will find the **Gents** has room for 2 seated, 6 standing, 4 abluting with what I first took to be little packets of sugar laid out on the basins. What part does sugar play in toileteering I tried to fathom. But no, sugar was not their contents – useful little shoeshine cloths it was. In the **Ladies**, 2 cubicles, 3 wash-basins, prints on the wall, armchairs, fresh flowers on the dressing tables and rare full-length dress-mirrors.

These Loos of the Rubens, while being a civilised alternative to those of Victoria Station, may also be an attractive alternative to those Toileteers who don't get asked to the Royal Loos in the Palace on the other side of the road.

But I still can't understand why train travellers need to visit loos on station platforms in the first place, rather than use the free loos provided on trains. Is it just something about the English that they prefer doing things in groups rather than solo?

___

STOP PRESS

Since this Guide started going to press a new and at present amazingly clean and modern **Gents** has opened on Victoria Station beneath the very clearly marked British Caledonian offices – approximately opposite the entrance to Platform 15. There are walls in stainless steel and bright red formica, 36 urinals the like of which you've never seen, like giant sauce-pans set into the walls, at least 20 hand-basins each with just one uni-water tap, and goodness knows how many cubicles (press button flushes to boot). This is a 10p loo, the only one so far with change machines at its entrance in case you haven't got a 10p on you. Amazing full-length steel swing doors which swing when you feed them your 10p, looking rather, I imagine, like going into San Quentin prison.

On the debit side, there are 4 video-cameras in these loos, covering all standing, all abluting Toileteers. It is a sad note on the age we live and go toileteering in that the authorities consider these necessary, but, such is the abuse of loos by some, there they are.

___

THE LOOS OF WESTMINSTER

The loos of The Tate Gallery
Millbank

These are on the lower ground floor near the restaurant. In the **Gents,** accommodations for 5 art-loving Toileteers

seated, 10 standing, and 7 washing their hands or brushes. In the **Ladies**, 8 small studios and 5 basins – not a single picture on the wall of either. The only rooms in the entire Gallery thus unadorned. It is ridiculous – nay, insulting – that Toileteers should be so discriminated against. There are just as many art-lovers among them as among any other group of persons in Britain – in fact, more so amongst Toileteers, as witness the walls and backs of doors that they themselves ornament in other loos they visit. And here, the only concession that the Trustees of the Gallery makes to them is to provide non-absorbent paper beside the lavatory basins because, presumably, it's easier to draw on.

In fact, this omission to decorate the walls of the Toileteers quarters here is doubly ridiculous when one considers that the Trustees are always bemoaning the lack of wall space they have to display the many masterpieces they are still required to keep in storage. So I remind them, I plead with them, I implore them to make use of these colourless walls in the loos and turn them into additional small Galleries they can be proud of, and which Toileteers from all over the world will want to visit. (Failing that, I wouldn't be averse to doing a mural in the Gents myself. How about Sandra Blow for the Ladies?).

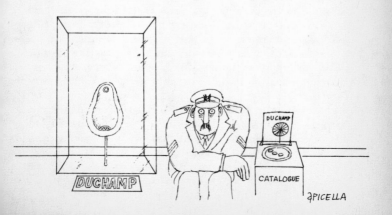

DUCHAMP

DUCHAMP

CATALOGUE

apicella

The Seats of Power – The loos of
The Houses of Parliament

Ken Livingstone after three weeks in this place still hadn't discovered the loos, even though he had the advantage of being able to open doors marked *For Members Only*, so it's doubtful if mere Commoners fare much better. But anyway, they have to get inside the building first, which is not always so simple.

Ask a policeman at the entrance to the Commons if you can just visit a loo and he will say, 'Certainly not', and direct you to the public loos at nearby Westminster Pier. Ask him when Parliament isn't sitting and there must be all those vacant seats and he'll still tell you the same.

Go to the House of Lords and ask the person at the door there – for all I know it's a Lord – and he will direct you to the just perceptibly nearer Queen Elizabeth Conference Hall across the road from Westminster Abbey. The only way to visit the loos there is to have a friend who's a Lord who will vouch for you, or, if you can contain yourself that long, just wait until you're made a Lord yourself.

The correct and proper way to visit the loos of the Commons is in fact to send a letter to your local MP asking if you may visit them on such and such a date, and in return he should send you a permit so to do. Alternatively you may join the queue of Japanese and other Toileteers waiting outside the St. Stephens entrance to the House to be admitted to the Strangers Gallery. A notice from the Sergeant at Arms at the head of the queue advises that Strangers joining the queue are admitted only as '*vacancies occur*' – Mondays to Thursdays not normally before 4.15 p.m., Friday before 10 a.m. '*And when*,' it continues, '*matters of special interest are being debated, there may be a long delay before seats become available.*'

However, when at last it is your turn to enter the building, there is still no rushing straight to the loo. There are persons and machines to investigate your body and your belongings – airport security style – for these proud guardians of our heritage do not want persons carrying concealed cameras gaining access to their loos, nor persons bearing weapons with which any of the porcelain fittings might be defaced. The search is thorough, and still at the end of it the patient Toileteer is not yet free to visit his goal. He must fill in his name and address on a form which, after it is stamped, thus making him eligible to use the loos of the Houses of Parliament, will go to be catalogued with the countless thousands of other forms which assiduous clerks look after in the nether-regions of the building, and which form the most complete record in the world of British and Foreign Toileteers.

Now the Toileteer may go through the ancient formality of being ushered into the Gallery where below him MPs or Lords debate, and from where at last he can ask the very spendidly dressed man in charge for permission to visit the loos.

AAAARRGH

If he is a **Gent** he is sent all the way back to the main entrance of the House, shown through a small unmarked doorway giving access to a small stone nave – barely 20-foot high at its centre (whereas almost every other room the Toileteer will have visited in the building has been 60 to 100 foot high) with accommodations for 1 Toileteer seated, 3 standing and 2 abluting. Nothing very special about the fittings at all, just good plain democratic plumbing.

And if the Toileteer is a **Lady** she will be directed to a room not quite so far removed from her Gallery as the Gents, with a statue of William Pitt by its entrance, and inside it a lot of pale blue tiling, 3 cubicles and 3 hand-basins. My Inspector of Ladies was smiled at by Norman Tebbitt and 'Something Hadderseley' as she came out of the loo – where else could that happen?

The loos of Victoria Embankment

1. The loos of Westminster Pier

Not visible from the roadway these are set into the river wall in the shadow of Big Ben. In the **Gents**, seats for 6, standing room for 9 (including – which makes the premises very special – for 4 Dwarfs), and with 3 exceptionally well-lit mirrored hand-basins. In the **Ladies** only 3 cubicles and 2 hand-basins. Much patronised by seafaring persons about to make the river trip to the Tower and Greenwich.

2. The loos of The Tattershall Castle Paddlesteamer

Down the gang-plank, follow the signs aft below-decks you will find small port-holed premises for both sexes. Their floors at a considerable tilt and a gentle swaying motion accompanying the experience. Last visits, 2.00 a.m.

3. The loos of The Hispaniola Restaurant Ship

Similar to those of the Tattershall Castle but smarter.

4. The loos of The Royal Horse Guards Hotel

This is part of that great French chateau style building called Whitehall Court in the Embankment Gardens, its entrance off Northumberland Avenue.

For Toileteers of both sexes, clean, adequate, pleasantly forgettable premises. Special Feature: in the **Gents**, machine dispensing Anadin (insert 2x10p).

Among famous Toileteers of the past who used this room before it was modernised (claims the hotel) were Gladstone, Lord Kitchener, Grand Duke Michael of Russia, Bernard Shaw and H. G. Wells.

THE LOOS SOUTH OF THE RIVER

The loos of Waterloo Station

Opposite Platform 18 are those labelled for **GENTLEMEN & BARBERS** advertising Toilets 10p, Showers £1. You pay down the stairs at a turnstile which, as I moved to go through it, gave me a vicious underkick in the groin, virtually impaling me until an attendant arrived to correct the machine's malfunctioning and so release me. Once safe inside there is a great deal of standing room as well as 23 numbered seats (which may not be booked in advance). Also 3 seats which – it must be on account of the great number of Barbers who patronise the establishment – if you use make you prey to being attacked by persons with scissors trying to shear off all your hair. There is also the Annexe which is sometimes open during rush hours, or sometimes just when this part is being cleaned. EXTRAS: two electric razors for use at 30p each, one trilingual automatic shoe polisher which takes francs and marks as well as 10ps, and rooms with a shower for £1 – the only snag here being, as the attendant admitted, 'we don't know actually when we'll be getting any towels in.'

The **NO SMOKING LADIES** establishment next door has 31 numbered 10p cabins, 15 hand basins and Mrs Routh says she thinks the large lady crawling round the room on all fours was probably the attendant. £1 shower rooms here also; and on station level facilities for Disabled Toileteers and Nursing Mothers.

An economic alternative to both these establishments exists in the only privately-owned part of Waterloo Station, the enterprising and very French-looking **Café de Piaf** down the great staircase opposite Platform 3. The really amazing fact about this place is that it used to be the main Gents at Waterloo and then in 1986 was converted to what it is today. Obviously the management would prefer you to sample their other fares at the same time as you patronise their charming free loos, and I strongly suspect that once you do so you will end up as a regular of the establishment.

The loos de Piaf open at noon, last visits 11.00 p.m.

The loos of The South Bank

There are loos at the National Theatre, but they prefer you to use them only just before or during the intervals of performances.

There are loos at the National Film Theatre, but to avail yourself of them you're meant to produce your Membership Card.

There are loos in the Hayward Gallery but to visit them you must pay the admission fee to whatever exhibition is on – normally about £3, which might be a small deterrent to some Toileteers.

That leaves the loos of the Festival Hall (unless you're willing to patronise the only loos which are actually sign-posted in the area, the public Loos of Upper Ground situated under Waterloo Bridge, part of the smart free chain run by Lambeth Council and open, like all Lambeth loos, 7.00 a.m. to 11.00 p.m.).

So, the **loos of the Festival Hall**. All these loos were opened by HM King George VI accompanied by HM Queen Elizabeth on 3rd May 1951. They have worn well.

Working upwards from the Ground or Box Office level we have a **Gents** with a machine dispensing 50p books of stamps at its entrance, and inside, accommodation for 5 Toileteers seated, 8 standing and 8 abluting in the midst of much black marble. But no chair or desk on which to write the letters to which you could affix some of these stamps. A **Ladies** nearby with 6 cubicles, 5 hand-basins and also much black marble.

Above, on Level 1 of the Hall, by the Riverside Restaurant, another **Ladies**, in wood panelling – and very hot – with 6 hand-basins, 6 chairs (for resting, making up or attending to your correspondence) and 6 cubicles (but 1 marked Private – whose could this be? Who can afford to keep a Private Loo, like a Private Box, at one of the world's great Concert Halls to-day? – '*Yes, well, if you're going to the Festival Hall tonight, please do use my loo, I'll get the key sent round to you*'). No Gents on this level any longer as it's been given over for the use of Disabled Toileteers, and there's a sign directing **Gents** to the Loos on Level 2.

These, in the Main Foyer near the Pasta Bar, offer accommodation for 3 Toileteers seated, 7 standing, and 2 abluting; and are in the midst of what looks like a lot of reject marble. The **Ladies**, several miles away on the other side of the Foyer, has 5 cubicles, 6 hand-basins, a hat-stand, a drinking fountain and is almost completely wood-panelled in the style of a thirties liner (as opposed to a fifties festival).

There are other loos on Levels 3, 4, 5 and 6 of the Hall but normally are used only in the evenings – the acoustics are remarkably good in all of them.

The loos of The Anchor
Bankside SE1

It's all very confusing here, at London's second oldest inn. There's a very good small **Gents** off Mrs Thrale's Room on the ground floor, just 1 cubicle, 4 stalls, and 2 tiny hand-basins, which presumably is the loo Dr Johnson would have used upon his visits to Mrs Thrale. The nearby **Ladies**, believed to be the room that Boswell favoured, has 2 cubicles, 1 hand-basin and 3 olde lamps. Then upstairs, off what's now called Boswell's Bar, there's a **Gents** with 2 cubicles, 6 stalls, and 2 hand-basins which could have been the room Shakespeare used (there were no facilities at the Globe Theatre round the corner and many of the actors used the Anchor as their changing room), or it could have been the room that Samuel Pepys used and next door to it, the room now called Shakespeare's Dining Room could really have been the room that Shakespeare used; alternatively, this

could have been the room that Sir Christopher Wren used as from it there are excellent views of St Paul's. Or Wren might have used the adjacent **Ladies** with its creaking floor and beams and 3 cubicles and the 2 hand-basins with nail-brushes chained to their taps. This latter idiosyncracy could be a reflection on the sort of female Toileteers who visit the room nowadays, or it could be traditional, a reminder of the ladies who used to patronise the place when in the adjacent street there existed the great line of bordellos – the 'damp houses of entertainment' licensed annually by the Bishops of Winchester with all due solemnity.

Whatever, the past of these loos, with their dungeons and plague-pits beneath them, the Clink prison beside them, the bear-fighting going on all around them, quite apart from the famous and infamous Toileteers who once came to visit them, they make exciting premises to visit to-day. And odd things still do happen there, as the man behind the bar explained to us. '*Some nights when there should be no one in them you hear things moving around in them. Why, even some of the young ladies who work in the place is afraid to visit them and they won't visit them unless a male member of staff accompanies them.*' Could it really be, *haunted* loos? '*Phantom Toileteer Strikes Again.*' To arms the rest of us mere mortal Toileteers and flush him out!

The historic loos of The George Inn

77 Borough High Street

These loos, over 300 years old, are now owned by the National Trust. In the **Gents** off the ground floor bar, 1 cubicle, 3 stalls, 2 hand-basins and a 50p souvenir scroll you can pay for at the bar which tells you that both Shakespeare and Dickens experienced the room's hospitality. The ground floor **Ladies**, with 3 cubicles and 2 hand-basins, makes no such claims.

● ● ● ● ● ●

A slit in the wall of the alleyway opposite the George is the entrance to a mean, very old-fashioned set of **Gents** accommodations typical of many thus sited in distressed areas of the North of England (a cubicle, a stall, and, very surprisingly, 2 hand-basins, within). A sign nearby says that the Rotary Club of Bermondsey meet here every Monday at 1.00 p.m. I just wonder if it wasn't this one that both Shakespeare and Dickens patronised.

APICELLA

THE LOOS ALONG PICCADILLY

The loos of Fortnum & Masons
118 Piccadilly

The best one here is the **Ladies** on the 1st floor. 5 (or some-times 6) cubicles, 4 hand-basins with decent cotton towels, good mirroring, a chair, and a rather sweet attendant.

The **Gents** on the 3rd floor just beyond the selection of coloured wrapping papers in Stationery (but you needn't stop to purchase any) I found, in appearance, disappointingly public-looish and very un-Fortnumish. I think it's because of the particular floor and walls tiles used in the room's con-struction. But anyway, 2 hand-basins, 3 stalls and 2 cubicles with not unattractive doors.

Another set of small loos down some stairs off the non-smokers section of the Fountain Restaurant on the lower ground floor (more conveniently entered from Jermyn Street than Piccadilly). Again, rather disappointing. (These ones open Mon–Sat 9.30 a.m. to 11.30 p.m.).

The loos of The Museum of Mankind
Burlington Gardens, just by Burlington Arcade

The good free loos in the entrance hall of this impressive building – all old fittings, not yet old enough to be quaint, more English genteel-shabby old – make a good alternative to having to pay £20 for a plate of pasta across the road at Cecconi's just to get into its loos.

The loos of The Royal Academy
Burlington House

Up the main staircase inside the front doors, **Gents** turn immediately left, **Ladies** right. Both, while clean, are totally dull and featureless. Not even one picture on the walls between them. A critically more rewarding alternative if you plan to spend much time toileteering in this area might be to join the Friends of the Royal Academy (yearly subscription around £20) which, the brochure says, entitles you to 'use of the Friends Room'.

The disappointing little loos of The Ritz

The **Gents**, up its own staircase to the left before the Palm Court, is a funny little marble and mosaic room sandwiched all on its own between the ground and first floors of the Hotel. I listed its contents as: 3 hand-basins with a stock of proper soaps and towels, 1 Refectory Chair, 2 Hooks on the wall, and 2 toilet seats with, beside each, a boxed labelled 'For your Convenience' (or it may have been 'For your Protection') and claiming to contain Disposable Paper Toilet Seat Covers.

The box had many baffling instructions on it explaining how to draw the Disposables out and what to do with them then, but at the end of two minutes my cubicle was littered like the floor of an unsuccessful Japanese Oregami factory – there was just no way I could work out how to turn these folded up covers into the shape they were meant to attain. And there was no attendant present to ask for help. So I stuffed it all into my pockets and left. (Then I forgot it was in my pockets and at lunch it all fell out).

Mrs Routh's notes on the **Ladies** of the Ritz are almost indecipherable. Through the same swing door from Piccadilly and turn right *down* some small stairs. 'Very tiny and clean', read her notes, '5 hand-basins, a picture and a Japanese lady attendant'. If that really was all, it does seem to leave a lot to be desired.

The old-world loos of Browns Hotel ★ ★

21–24 Dover Street – or Albemarle Street, off Piccadilly
The **Gents** (like the Ladies, down the stairs outside the St George's Bar on the ground floor) is a splendid survival of gracious living. An old-fashioned club-like atmosphere about its spacious many-mirrored and much-mahoganyed outer room, old-carpeted and with four large marble and mahogany wash-basins, with its writing desk and magazines to read and its really old-fashioned padded Weighing Chair surrounded with more conventional easy chairs for friends you may wish to invite to your weighing. And, I forgot to mention, beside the basins a splendid array of after-shave lotions, talcum powders, nail files, tweezers, brushes and

even stain removing cloths for you to use – increasingly rare these days. The inner room, equally spacious and with facilities for 4 seated and 4 standing Toileteers. And yet another room, with just one chair and one barber, where gentlemen may be manicured and hairdressed. The attendant here is to be complimented on the loo he keeps.

In the **Ladies** next door, a cheerful lady to greet you with a 'Good Morning Madame' as you enter, to provide brushes, combs and pins for those without them, or to minister to those for whom the chaise-longue is there and who may have been taken faint.

The loos of Langan's Brasserie
Stratton House, Stratton Street, off Piccadilly

The **Ladies**, upstairs, spacious, carpeted, some fine original paintings on its walls, and with 3 cubicles, 4 hand-basins, is a must for Toileteers in this part of the world.

The **Gents**, down the stairs immediately to the right inside the front entrance, has 4 very fine hand-basins set in a rare black marble, fresh carnations in vases decorating them. Also accommodation for 3 Toileteers standing, 1 seated, and 1 on the phone. An open adjacent room is where Peter Langan is temporarily housing his Collection of Old English Coat Hangers.

The loos of The Mayfair Hotel
Stratton Street, off Piccadilly

Turn left inside the main entrance from Stratton Street and go up the stairs. A **Ladies** Powder Room with 2 cubicles, 2 hand-basins. A **Gents** from which someone had removed the *entire* contents, leaving it just a bare space with cement walls and marks where once there had been fittings. Seeking other relief I went downstairs, and down more stairs, and still more, and then through kitchens and past subterranean ball-rooms, and up stairs, and up more stairs, and eventually found a corridor which led out into Berkeley Street – and along this corridor the room I sought. According to my notes, in it were all the usual requirements plus two elegant long couches. I wonder if it was the Gents I visited? Indeed, was I even in the Mayfair Hotel?

THE LOOS OF ST. JAMES'S

It is difficult if you are not a Member, wearing a tie to prove it, or Guest of a Member, of one of the old-established and prestigious St. James's Loos – annual membership of which is as astronomically large financially as the Waiting List to join is long – to find any loo at which you will be welcome in this very select area of London. There are just a very few establishments where the needy Toileteer will not be looked at askance (and where there are also loos for Ladies):

The loos of Christies, Fine Art
8 King Street
Through the front door and they're situated on that level in a cranny to the left of the staircase. In the **Gents**, normally, 2 cubicles, (but watch out, less than six foot head clearance), 3 stalls, 2 hand-basins. In the **Ladies**, normally, 4 cubicles, 3 hand-basins. No reserve on any item in these rooms, and Viewing Days are advertised in the daily press.

apicell9

The loos of Dukes Hotel
35 St. James's Place
The **Gents**, downstairs, is a little gem, absolutely gleaming and offering accommodations for 1 Toileteer seated, 2 standing, 2 abluting. The **Ladies** on the ground floor offers 2 cubicles, 2 hand-basins, some very good soaps and a mass of flowers. But the real triumph of these loos is the little Emergency Sewing Kit they offer Toileteers, so if you're planning to lose a button make sure you do it in this area.

The loos of The Stafford Hotel
St. James's Place

Gents, through the lounge and towards the Cocktail Bar, 1 cubicle, 3 stalls, 3 basins, but really too cramped for more than one Toileteer at a time to make use of these facilities. A **Ladies** with more space (but not for Gents) nearer to the hotel entrance.

● ● ● ● ● ●

If it is your pleasure to approach a loo by first ascending a very grand staircase indeed then think up some reason why you should visit the Jamaica Tourist Board upstairs in Jamaica House at the top of St. James's. Tiny little loos but, oh, the grandeur that surrounds you as you make your way to them.

The loos of St. James's Park
1.   The Loos of the Mall

Cunningly concealed in the bushes opposite the road leading to St James's Palace some prosaic little brick buildings house free loos which are amongst the most picturesquely situated in the capital. Surrounded by well-kept flower beds, approached up cobbled paths covered in great bowers of greenery the furnishings are adequate if pedestrian – a boon to' picnicking Toileteers. In the **Gents**, accommodation for 5 seated, 8 standing and 3 abluting Toileteers. In the **Ladies**, 11 cubicles, 3 wash-basins. Very separate entrances to each set of loos.

2.   The Loos of Horseguards Parade

In the bushes opposite the parade ground these loos are every bit as romantically sited as those of the Mall. The **Gents** has room for 10 standing, 3 seated and 2 abluting. The **Ladies**, 7 cubicles, 3 wash-basins and a certain amount of graffiti – not necessarily written by a female hand.

These loos also act as an overflow on big nights at Number Ten Downing Street just across the road.

THE LOOS OF PARK LANE

The loos of The Inter-Continental
Hyde Park Corner

Turn right through the main entrance and up a few stairs through the bar. In the **Gents**, very smart accommodations for 2 Toileteers seated, 8 standing and 3 abluting. In the equally smart **Ladies**, 3 cubicles, 3 hand-basins, an ante-room with 2 chairs and mirrors.

Another set of loos, almost theatrical in their decor and lighting, down the Victor-Haddesley-hunting-print-lined walls of the stairs at entrance to the Coffee Room.

The luxury loos of The Inn On The Park
Hamilton Place

Up the great stairs inside the main entrance and turn right. The **Ladies**, displaying the Kimberley Clark Certificate of Excellence for having been Britain's Best Ladies Hotel Wash-room in 1986, is very elegant indeed; 8 cubicles with brass fittings, 8 hand-basins with good soaps and plants around them, 3 oyster-pink marble dressing tables with mirrors in a carpeted area – and the kindly Portuguese attendant has been in them for 15 years. The **Gents**, with ash-trays on both sides of its cubicles, and by its 8 stalls and 7 hand-basins is obviously a great favourite among smoking Toileteers. Flow-ering plants on the hand-basins too, and bottles of Highland Spring Natural Mineral Water.

These are places impossible to fault except for their compa-rative dullness.

The loos of The Dorchester

The most conveniently placed for the needy Toileteer are the small ones to the right of the front lobby after the lifts. In the **Gents**, two of each expected requirement – attendant standing by to hand you a towel at the hand-basin, and Choice of Tooth-picks or Match-boxes as a souvenir of your visit. In the **Ladies**, 3 cubicles, 4 hand-basins (real soap and real linen towels), real fresh flowers and hand-cream, a proper dressing table.

The loos of Grosvenor House

Park Lane

They're very grand, as you might expect. Nearer to the Park Lane (Ballroom) entrance than Park Street. The **Gents**, one of the few rooms in town which smells like an old-fashioned Gents should smell – of fine soaps and subtle scents – is immaculate. 3 cubicles with choice of papers, and 5 hand-basins, 2 of which the attendant always has ready filled with hot water, and beside the basins, lotions and sprays and Malvern waters. The **Ladies** has 5 luxurious cubicles, 6 luxurious hand-basins, and 7 luxurious dressing tables and stools.

I would *expect* Grosvenor House to have all this. I just wish that the travelling Toileteer could also find it and be wonderfully surprised by it, in Bermondsey or at South Kensington Underground station.

THE LOOS OF MAYFAIR

The loos of Shepherd Market

The phone numbers of some of the privately-owned ones are displayed on the notice boards here – nearly all for Gents and with fairly exorbitant Admission charges.

A clean, cheap and safe alternative might be . . .

The loos of The Curzon Cinema
Curzon Street

In the foyer just beyond the box office and sweet counter – but before you actually get to see what's on the screen, so you don't really need a ticket for these loos.

Gents, very smart with white marble floors and walls, 2 hand-basins, 4 stalls, and 1 cubicle which also sports a hand-basin.

Ladies, equally smart, hunting prints on its marble walls, 5 cubicles, 3 hand-basins with 5 soaps.

The loos of The Connaught Hotel ★
Carlos Place

These are immaculate – not ostentatious, not even splendid – just exactly what the loos of a good hotel should be. Somehow, a rather grand country house atmosphere about them, which is totally lacking in most other great London hotels especially those of American ownership. Straight ahead through the lobby, the **Gents** has accommodations for 2 rather grand Toileteers seated, 4 standing, and 3 abluting – at marble and mahogany hand-basins on which the scrubbing brushes are changed every day. There are also in the room 2 spitoons – unless they're free-standing ashtrays – and supplies of Alka Seltzer, Anadin, Aspirin, Optrex, and Odol Mouthwash – no reflection on what's served in the Restaurant I'm sure, but just in case you're an addict of any of these products.

In the adjacent **Ladies**, well, read my Inspector of Ladies notes: '2 shell-shaped sinks (Crabtree and Evelyn soaps), pink towels matching the pink wall covering, mirrors edged in silk rope, 3 cubicles with brass and mahogany fittings and each with a real window and the most heavenly curtains, masses of fake flowers and one real potted plant'.

The loos of Claridges

Through the main Brook Street entrance and turn right, Ladies through an archway on the ground floor, Gents a little further on and down a very grand staircase. In the cubicles of both loos old-fashioned pull-up handles to operate the flush. In the **Gents** some beautiful tiling and mosaics, just 2 cubicles, 5 stalls, and 4 hand-basins – no one to fill one for me on the occasion of my visit which I thought was a bad mark – 1 unchained hairbrush and comb, 1 unchained clothes brush, 1 bottle of Listerine with a wine glass beside it. In the **Ladies**, stuffed armchairs and potted plants, 3 cubicles, 4 black marble hand-basins *and* someone to fill them for you and hover around you with a towel, sweet-smelling soaps, free face powders, a flask of water with glasses, and another room with pink buttoned chairs. What you would expect of the place.

apicella

THE LOOS OF BERKELEY SQUARE

(That is not a loo in the middle of the Square; it's where the gardener keeps his tools.)

The loos of Annabel's ★

44 Berkeley Square

There are two disadvantages about these loos: they're not available for use in the daytime, and the Annual Subscription for Membership of them has now gone up to £500. Apart from that, they are very exceptional loos.

In the **Gents**, its walls decorated with Chinese Share Certificates, as well as those of Panama and other slightly suspect countries, 1 cubicle, 3 stalls, 2 hand-basins and a charming Attendant who can supply most other things. Toileteers who have not visited the premises for some time may be surprised to see the compact Press Association machine in one corner which has replaced the old ticker-tape one. It provides a steady stream of up-to-the-minute news of interest to Toileteers and is also alleged to produce more volume of paper than is consumed daily in the one cubicle. At the same time they will be saddened to note the absence from the walls of the H. M. Bateman cartoon they used to look at when standing at the stalls – believed removed from the premise by a felonious Toileteer under cover of his overcoat on the night of April 14, 1987.

If it is difficult to understand on hygenic grounds the mysterious printed request that Toileteers should wear dark suits when visiting these Loos, one must bear in mind that Annabel's loos do have one of the most distinguished clienteles of any set of Loos in London, and it could come as a shock, capable of incapacitating him, for a Serious and Distinguished Toileteer to find himself of an evening in the proximity of another Toileteer not wearing full Toileteering uniform.

The **Ladies** – first door on the right once you're inside Annabel's – has 2 cubicles, 2 hand-basins, a good sprinkling of perfumes and such-like – and, of course, Mabel, in charge of the cloaks as she has been for the last 25 years, knowing the names of all her thousands of Ladies, there to sew on their buttons, provide pills for their headaches, and – what she's best-known for – to give them counsel. Much more an Aunt than an Attendant is Mabel.

The loos of The Lansdowne Club

9 Fitzmaurice Place

Turn right inside the entrance-way and take the stairs which lead down to the Swimming Pool. The **Gents** is approached through flimsy half-length curtains. In one room are accommodations for 6 Toileteers seated and 6 standing. In another room are 4 hand-basins (2 displaying nail-brushes which are chained to the wall), a table with 2 hair-brushes which are chained and padlocked to the wall, and elsewhere

APICELLA

there are 4 shoe-shine brushes also chained to the wall (but masses of loose tins of shoe polish). Well, I was thinking, it certainly shows the sort of clientele they have – or must once have had – in this place. And to cap it all I then stumbled into another room which had 20 long chains chained to the wall. The only places I've ever seen this before are the sort of places where they expect troublesome prisoners. What you have to do at the Lansdowne Club to get into this category I really don't know. Be caught trying to make off with a shoe-shine brush perhaps.

There is a **Ladies** loo nearby here. My Inspector's comments are a little baffling though (or perhaps nothing is baffling once you've come across all those chains in the Gents): 'All luminous green,' she has written in her notes, '2 cubicles, 1 lady with no clothes on, lots of showers, and Cocktails'. It sounds a lot more fun in the Ladies anyway.

Another very grand **Ladies** at this establishment half way up the stairs which lead from the foyer to the Savage Club. Carpeted, chintz curtains, writing desk and chair, kidney-shaped dressing tables as well as the usual cubicle and hand-basin. And, writes my Inspector, 'opens on to a bathroom overlooking people in the downstairs lounge taking afternoon tea'. I wonder if she meant ballroom not bathroom.

The loos of The English-Speaking Union
37 Charles Street

In the **Ladies**, past the staircase on the ground floor, 4 cubicles, 4 hand-basins sharing 2½ bits of soap, a good long make-up mirror and stool.

The **Gents**, downstairs, with 1 room marked Shower, elsewhere accommodation for 4 English-Speaking Toileteers seated, 4 standing, 6 abluting – but, and now this is getting ridiculous, the clothes brush *is chained to the wall*. And outside the room are another 20 chains chained to the wall. What's going on in Mayfair these days?

THE LOOS OF BOND STREET

The loos of The Westbury Hotel
Conduit Street

Turn left in the lobby and you will find the **Ladies**. I will reproduce my Inspector of Ladies notes: 'Immensely elegant, *our* bedroom material on walls and stool covers. Beautiful real matching flowers. 2 sinks with marble tops, mirrors, shelves and good lighting. Real linen towels, nice soaps, and a glass for a drink.'

After the Ladies and down some stairs can be found the **Gents** – in their entrance is a spectacular shoe-shine chair – within can be found accommodation for 6 standing, 3 seated and 6 abluting. Boxes of tissues and individual 'linen-like' towels abound – but the toilets were disappointingly scruffy – with used tissues and towels eveywhere and pans left unflushed. Shame on The Westbury!

The loos of Sotheby's
34 New Bond Street

Up a small staircase past the Catalogue Kiosk. In the **Gents**, Lot No 101, 1 Royal Doulton lavatory basin; Lot No 102, 2 Porcelain Stalls (School of Doulton); Lot No 103, 1 Hand-basin (No maker's name but probably mid 20th C); Lot No 104, 2 Roller Towel Dispensers (some towelling slightly soiled). Estimated value of these fittings *in toto*, £800–£1200.

In the **Ladies** nearby, Lot No 201, 2 cubicles with traditional fittings, approx 206 cms by 96 cms by 96 cms; Lot No 202, 2 hand-basins, unsigned, glazed enamel on porcelain, 65 cms by 28 cms by 18 cms; Lot No 203, Contemporary drinking water tap with set of contemporary plastic cups. Estimated value *in toto* £700–£1000.

The loo at Asprey's
165 New Bond Street

It's not marked but it's through the doorway on the lst floor amongst Clocks and Chronometers. The trouble is there's nothing to let you know whether the small premises is occupied or not. Seated just outside the room on a George III mahogany settee in Hepplethwaite's French manner c. 1770 and very reasonably priced at £9450, I watched Toileteers attempt to enter the room. I heard them banging on inner doors, heard them being repulsed by voices from within, watched them re-emerge and take an intense interest in the English mahogany 8-day regulator c. 1820, also very reasonably priced I thought at £24,000. When such time as they saw someone leave the room and so allow them to lose their interest in clocks and chronometers and make a further dash for it. There's just 1 cubicle, 1 hand-basin and a lot of cupboards inside, nothing to really excite the sophisticated Toileteer.

THE LOOS OF OXFORD STREET

The loos of The Cumberland Hotel
Marble Arch

They exist, on the ground floor through the Coffee Shop, and by the stairs at the entrance to the Carvery. Adequate, but just not very memorable.

The loos of Marks & Spencer
458 Oxford Street

There are none available to the public (certain members of which body might well take advantage of their shelter to clothe themselves in the 12 pairs of panties, 6 sweaters and 14 dresses they had just shoplifted). We were recommended to visit those of Selfridges.

The loos of Selfridges
Oxford Street

The **Ladies** in the basement, through Glassware, has 10 cubicles, 7 pale apricot hand-basins, masses of good mirrors with good lighting and a *huge* number of Ladies using and waiting to use these facilities.

The **Gents** in the basement, seemingly miles away on the other side of London, through TV Sets, appears to have 14 cubicles, 6 hand-basins, 7 stalls, and in an annexe, another 12 hand-basins. A massive place in new formica and wood but with very few customers.

Another Gents is alleged to be on the 1st floor, but I never found it. Yet another **Gents** is on the 4th floor near the Lifts leading to the top of the Shop Restaurant, accommodation for 4 Toileteers seated, 4 standing and 4 abluting. Very clean but frosted glass in the windows which overlooked Oxford Street. Speciality of this loo: a Palmist – Madame Diaz, who offers to read your Palm for £4.50 (but not on Fridays. Whose loo is she working then I wonder?).

On the other side of Madame Diaz, a **Ladies** with 2 vast rooms, good views of Oxford Street through windows that have chain mail curtains, 12 cubicles, 4 hand-basins and 2 attendants.

And yet another **Ladies** just below on the 3rd floor. An excitable group of mostly non-English-speaking Gents was being ejected from it at the time of our visit, apparently Glassmasters from Czechoslovakia who had arrived to exhibit their wares elsewhere on the floor and had thought this room was for them (that was their story anyway). My Inspector of Ladies says that this loo has an endless number of cubicles, endless halls of mirrors and rows of basins she thinks run right up Oxford Street, and a Baby's Comfort Area.

Marks and Sparks, please copy.

The loos of The Selfridge Hotel
Orchard Street

Upstairs through the slightly mock olde-world Lounge, good mock olde-world loos for all. Carpets and chairs in the Ladies and a very *peaceful* atmosphere.

The loos of Debenhams, D. H. Evans, John Lewis, and BHS
Oxford Street

They exist, they're free, and they're very dull.

The loos of Oxford Circus

These are inconveniently situated and dangerously approached down steps on a traffic island in the middle of Upper Regent Street just above Oxford Circus. 99% of the thousands of persons sheltering on the island at any given moment are not in fact Toileteers, but pedestrians just attempting to cross the road. In rush hours many of them prefer to give up their pedestrianism and take shelter downstairs in the loos until the traffic abates – and fortunately these loos are well equipped to cater for crowds. In the **Ladies**, 15 cubicles, 16 pink and yellow hand-basins (and one 15p room for those who prefer to wash their hands in privacy), 1 mirror, 1 10p weighing machine, 2 attendants (one singing while the other polishes the piping), a 20p machine dispensing pre-pasted tooth-brushes, and another machine – presumably for those who just can't face the road upstairs until the traffic disappears in the small hours – giving out Overnight Vanity Packs. In the **Gents**, only 6 cubicles, but 12 of the latest stainless steel stalls, 8 little centre-situated hand-basins, a 10p weighing machine, and other machines dispensing pre-pasted tooth-brushes, Durex Featherlites, and Overnight Travel Packs.

The loos of The Berners Hotel

(*now The Ramada Hotel*) *10 Berners Street*

Anyone looking for the once famous loos of this once famous hotel is reminded that they are now the loos of the Ramada Hotel – downstairs near the Berners Rooms – and showing few signs of any fame to-day. (4 cubicles, 7 stalls, 3 basins in the **Gents**, too many ladies in the **Ladies** to count how many of anything).

apicella

THE LOOS OF ST. MARYLEBONE & BAKER STREET

The loos of Marylebone Station

These must rank – at any rate, at the time of our inspection – as nearly the nastiest loos in London.

The **Gents**, quite ghastly, as though a mad Dr Beeching had been let loose on it. 6 cubicles, 3 of them with doors and lavatory seats, 3 of them without doors and lavatory seats. 2 stalls and a space on the walls where a 3rd had been. 4 other stalls on another wall. And 1 tiny hand-basin with no soap and a broken down electric hand-dryer. Elsewhere 2 doors marked Staff Only – I can only hope they fare better than visitors to this abject establishment.

The **Ladies** is worse. At the time of our inspection there was a blackboard erected by the Station Police at its entrance appealing for information regarding a 'white male with an Irish accent' who had committed a 'Serious Sexual Assault upon an Elderly Woman Attacked in the Ladies Toilet' some few days prior to our visit. A group of female Toileteers was clustered around it deciding whether or not to enter the premises. Had they done so they would have found 10 cubicles in various states of disrepair, 3 hand-basins, an ancient incinerator, an untended Attendant's box, and what my Inspector describes as 'a lot of very spooky hiding places'. Oh dear.

The loos of Marylebone Magistrates Court

In the Waiting Room off Court 1, just inside the entrance from Marylebone Road, is a door marked GAOLER which is presumably the Gaoler's Loo, another door marked **Men** which contains 2 cubicles, 2 stalls, and 1 hand-basin, and another door marked **Women** which opens on to a cubicle with a museum piece of a brush holder in it. There are Notices pasted around the waiting-room announcing who's appearing in Court that day and from it you will realise that any other Toileteer who joins you in a Loo is probably a Witness for – or a Relative of – someone had up for Violent Behaviour, Possession of Drugs, Obstruction of Police,

Attempted Deception, Handling Stolen Goods, Aggravated Burglary or Grievous Bodily Harm. Don't worry, the loos for all those persons are elsewhere.

The prohibitive loos of Baker Street

The nearest Loos to Baker Street Station seem to be the Westminster ones on the other side of Baker Street – under the road – roughly opposite the Planetarium. In the **Gents,** 8 free cubicles, 12 stainless steel stalls, 4 hand-basins, sockets for electric shavers (why is Kensington so down on shaving and Westminster so open-minded about it?). If you read the Westminster Bye-laws displayed here you find Bye-Law 4 '*No 2 or more persons shall enter or occupy a water closet compartment without first having obtained the consent of the attendant on duty in the Convenience at that time.*' And Bye-Law 5, '*No person shall unreasonably prevent the use of any part of the convenience by other persons.*' Does this mean that a Toileteer who has obtained 'the consent of the attendant on duty' can barge into a cubicle you are using and try to occupy it without your being able to complain? Other Notices in this loo say No Dogs (I should hope not too), No Consumption of Alcohol, Loitering Prohibited, and Beware of Pickpockets.

In the nearby **Ladies** there are 7 free numbered cubicles (but numbered with No.1 out of order; 8; 5; 4; 3; 1; and 2 of which were Out of Order), 4 old-fashioned hand-basins and hand-dryers six feet above the floor which are quite useful for drying hair even if your hands won't reach them.

The mysterious loos of Paddington Street

They're situated in one of London's least-known parks which bears much evidence of once having been a cemetery. In fact many Toileteers mistake one particular large mausoleum for the loos, whereas the real loos are in a charming cottage-type building right beside the pavement. They're labelled Seymour Indoor Leisure Centre which seems a bit odd, and on the occasion of our visit they were shut because, we were told, the attendant was mowing the grass around them in the park. I would welcome more information about these loos from local Toileteers.

The loos of The Sherlock Holmes Hotel
Baker Street

In the **Gents** – down the staircase near the bar which serves drinks with names like The Mummy's Curse, Moriarty's Martini, and The Deerstalker Cap – then down more stairs, then through four different doors – expecting to be hit on the head by a sinister Chinese as I opened each one of them, or at least to find lying behind it the corpse of a sinister Chinese – his facial features bright green and almost unrecognisable because of the terrifying effects of the poisons administered to him by a bogus barman upstairs – and finally into a room which had in it 3 sinister cubicles, 5 sinister stalls and 4 sinister hand-basins. My sinister cubicle had no clues in it concerning its previous occupant, the great flush having wiped it clean of any incriminating evidence; but I knew that in the cubicle next to me there had been a one-handed American with false teeth and a limp who had recently visited Madame Tussauds –

'My God, Routh, how did you know that?'

'Because, my dear Watson, I saw him washing his hand and his false teeth in the hand-basin beside me, and just before he limped away, he threw his ticket of admission to Madame Tussauds into the trash can.'

In the **Ladies** near here, 3 rather dull cubicles, 3 extremely dull hand-basins.

★ ★ *The loos of the Wallace Collection*
Hertford House, Manchester Square

The **Gents** at the back of the building (turn right just before European Armour and go down the stairs) is without doubt – and despite the reason for its existence – one of the most beautiful rooms in London. This is because of the old Minton tiles, originally from Sir Richard Wallace's Smoking Room, with which its walls are faced. A plaque on one wall records that 'The Worshipful Company of Tylers and Brick-layers, awarded it its Tiling Award in 1981' – a little late in the day as most of the tiles date from 1874. There is spacious accommodation in the room for 3 Toileteers seated, 4 standing and 2 abluting – the hand-basins must be the

original ones, old marble set into faded mahogany, real
collectors pieces, worthy of space in the galleries upstairs.

The **Ladies**, also at the back of the building but on the
other side to the Gents, is almost as grand – tiled, with 2
cubicles, 4 hand-basins and an elegant chaise-longue for
Toileteers given to swooning and fainting.

The approach to these loos, the cloistered peace of the
courtyard that they surround, and the solicitude of their staff
make them paragons amongst the Loos of London. Entry to
them and to the Wallace Collection is absolutely free.
Monday to Saturdays open 10 to 5, Sundays 2 to 5.

The loos of Durrant's Hotel ★

George Street

Turn left inside the front entrance. The **Gents** on the ground
floor is just opposite the bar. A delightful room. 2 cubicles, 4
mirrored stalls, 3 good hand-basins each with its own new
bar of Pears soap, and over them a charming picture of the
Lambeth Patent Pedestal Combination Closet *'especially
adapted for places where such furnishings are liable to rough
usage . . . Strongly Recommended for Asylums.'* Also in the room
a very early electrical shoeshine machine, and another
machine which dispenses (insert 2x50p) packets of disposable
razors, Colgate tooth-paste and Paracetamol Tablets.

The **Ladies** nearby is a civilised carpeted room with 3
cubicles, 3 hand-basins and an Anadin dispenser.

St. Christopher's loos

St. Christopher's Place, Barrett Street, off James Street

Serving the pedestrian precinct and open-air cafes of St.
Christopher's Place these good little underground loos are
efficiently run by a lady who opted for a life in lavatories 18
years ago and during that time worked continuously at most
of Westminster Council's top loos.

In her **Gents**, room for 2 seated Toileteers, 5 standing and 3
abluting. Pre-pasted tooth-paste and Overnight Travel Pack
Machines.

In her **Ladies**, 4 cubicles, 3 hand-basins, 4 mirrors,
machines dispensing tooth-paste, tights, perfume and vanity

packs; and notices concerning Drugs, Fostering and the locations of the new automatic loos.

And what changes has this lady, now reaching the top of her profession, seen in all this time? All the massive old fittings and fixtures have been replaced; brass rails down stairs have been supplanted by chrome; and the system of having just one attendant for both loos which was introduced 4 years ago.

The loo of John Bell & Croyden
Chemists, *50 Wigmore Street*
It's not sign-posted but a charitable attendant directed me to it, down in the basement just by Incontinence Pants and Systems. I suspect it is for emergency use by more genuine customers than myself.

The loos of St. George's Hotel
Langham Place
These loos, approached by express lift to the 15th floor Summit Bar and Restaurant, may not be the highest loos in London, but they must be the highest loos with such incredible views – picture windows such as these possess not normally being part of any loo furnishings.

Through them the Toileteer looks out over half of London and, if not satisified by that he (or she) then wants to see the other, Western half, he (or she, or even both together) can repair to the adjacent Bar and look out of its windows. This is very civilised toileteering, and in addition there's cologne and Listermint and a shoeshine apparatus in the **Gents**, and various unguents and lotions in the **Ladies**.

The loos of Regent's Park
One of the most delightfully situated of all London loos is that off the Inner Circle at the entrance to Queen Mary's Rose Garden in the Park. You approach it through great ornamental wrought-iron gates, the scent of the surrounding roses and other flowers quite overwhelming you. No trace of the loos, but as you get nearer to where they lie, totally concealed by, and covered in greenery, you become aware of a

new and puzzling scent fighting with that of Queen Mary's roses. What strange growth, what luxuriant foliage produces this odour, you ask yourself? Only as you turn into the loos does it suddenly dawn on you it is that of the disinfectants that the diligent guardians of the premises lavish upon their gleaming floors and walls. The rooms themselves, apart from the traditional loo fittings, are two of the cleanest, plainest rooms in London, very great contrasts to the wealth of nature outside them.

There are other loos in the Park, near the Boating Lake, in the restaurant near the Open-Air Theatre, and of course, in the Zoological Gardens, but the admission charges to the Zoo are so exorbitant that no Toileteer except one of wildly independent means would dream of visiting them.

LOOS OF THE EUSTON ROAD

The loos of Euston Station

The **Gents** opposite the entrance to Platforms 1 and 2 has 20 5p cubicles, a row of stainless steel stalls, 12 hand-basins, a £1 Durex Featherlite dispenser and a rather unpleasant smell. There's a notice outside apologising for this and saying refurbishment is at hand. Open 24 hours.

The **Ladies** has 20 5p cubicles (many containing toileteers with all their luggage), 14 hand-basins, a drinking fountain, a nursing mother's room, and machines dispensing Vanity Packs, pre-pasted tooth-brushes and eau-de-cologne. Open 24 hours.

★ ★ The superloos of Euston Station

These are upstairs next to the Pullman Lounge which passengers with first-class tickets are entitled to use. And after all the nasty things I've been led to say about railway loos it's quite wonderful to find them. They're vast, spendidly decorated and with plate-glass windows overlooking all the roving hordes of the station.

To enjoy their basic facilities you pay 30p to the attendant at the box office outside their doorways – or £1.30 if you want a shower (entitling you to 20 minutes in it) or £1.30 if you want a bath (not meant to be longer than 30 minutes) – and he'll hand you the relevant ticket and towel. The 4 bathrooms I saw in the **Gents** could easily grace the grandest hotel, they're open 7.00 a.m. to 10.30 p.m., and the big rush for them is between 7 and 8 a.m. (from passengers off the Glasgow train), and again between 4 and 5 p.m. (builders cleaning up before returning to Manchester – which sounds a bit odd). Other features of the Gents, 10p automatic shoe-shine, 10p Brut and free razor sockets. Special features of the **Ladies**, the theatre dressing room type make-up mirrors, and hair-driers.

The loos of Friend's Meeting House

Friends House, Euston Road
Use the garden entrance of this great building – half Quaker

Church, half Quaker administrative offices – and go down to the basement near the No Smoking Restaurant. The **Gents** is vast with a good old-fashioned feel to it. 9 cubicles with Western-type swing doors, 20 king-size stalls, 18 centrally-situated (in the room) hand-basins on fine old iron stands and all draining into one communal open gutter which runs beneath them. The **Ladies** has 100 coat pegs (all empty, perhaps because of the sign hanging beside them 'This cloak-room is not under supervision. Personal property is left here at risk'), 5 Western style cubicles, each with a shelf on the wall for keeping handbags and personal property safe and dry, each with an amazing Unihygea Automatic Disinfectant and Deoderiser device attached to the cistern and which springs into action every time the loo is flushed. Also some hand-basins around. There is also a machine between these 2 loos which dispenses cheese and onion crisps and Mars Bars.

The loos of St Pancras

If only these loos alongside Platform 7 looked like the exterior of the mad red-brick building which houses them – but they don't, modernisation has taken its toll again. In the **Gents** 5 free cubicles (fair amount of Lonely Hearts graffiti on the back of the doors), 7 stalls, 3 hand-basins and a smell. In the **Ladies**, 5 cubicles, 2 hand-basins and a nursing mothers room.

The loos of Kings Cross Station

They're off Platform 8, together with one for the Disabled. In the **Gents** you pay 10p at a turnstile for the use of the facilities – 40p for a shower and washroom. Accommodations in one room for 5 Toileteers seated, 8 standing, 3 abluting and 2 showering. Accommodations in an annexe for 7 Toileteers seated, 12 standing, 4 abluting and 3 showering. A 20p pre-pasted toothbrush dispenser in one of the rooms.

In the **Ladies**, a similar 10p method of gaining entrance, and 9 cubicles, 13 hand-basins, 15 pegs, 2 showers, a 20p pre-pasted toothbrush dispenser and a 60p Vanity Pack machine (the Pack contains a Face Freshener, Shampoo, Moisturiser, Comb, Tooth-brush, Cotton-wool, Safety Pin, Hairgrips, and Emery Board). According to the Countometer Meter on the turnstile my Inspector was the 258 168th Toileteer to have visited the room that day. She was only there for five minutes but the Countometer was up to 258 192 when she left.

The loos of The British Museum

All the loos here are really very dull and pedestrian and I'm surprised that a place with the reputation that the British Museum has bothered to give them any space at all.

The prominent sign in the main entrance hall, 'Mediaeval Renaissance and Modern Collections Coin & Medal

Womens Lavatories' indicates the position of one **Ladies**, just to the right of the Great Staircase. The **Gents** off this hall is found down the stairs near the Information Desk. Another set of **Gents** and **Ladies** – walk left from the entrance hall towards the Coffee Shop and just after the Mummies, Bronzes of the Geometric Period and Collection of Greek Potties you will find them. And another set by Room 25 in the Egyptian Sculpture Gallery just by the aptly-positioned red granite Relief of Amenophis III (1430 B.C.).

But really, all these loos are of absolutely no interest at all to any but the most needy Toileteer.

THE LOOS OF SOHO

The loos of Great Marlborough Street Magistrates Court

Some bafflement here. There definitely are doors marked Men and Women in the waiting room which leads up to the sign saying Gaolers Enquiries, but they're both locked. And a request for a key at the first office inside the building simply produces the answer that they're kept locked up 'for security reasons' – are they afraid someone might steal the bar of soap? It's probably easier to cross the road and visit. . .

The multi-coloured public loos of Great Marlborough Street

. . . which also serve the Toileteers of Carnaby Street. In no public loos in London have so many coloured tiles been put together so amazingly. In the **Gents** 5 multi-coloured cubicles, 6 stalls, 4 hand-basins. In the **Ladies**, 5 pink and yellow cubicles, 4 tiny hand-basins set into mauve, yellow and black tiling, and, cunningly concealed in a room made of two-way mirror glass, an attendant. The whole dominated by a ceramic portrait of Sarah Duchess of Marlborough by Casey. This is believed to be a City of Westminster loo.

The loos of The Coach & Horses
Propr. **Norman Balon,** *29 Greek Street*

The attraction of these small cramped loos (**Gents** at the back of the room on the right, **Ladies** on the left) is that Jeffrey Bernard is one of the distinguished regular Toileteers who use them (the Gents that is) and also there's always the chance that on your way there you will come up against the calculated but entertaining rudeness of the celebrated proprietor.

The loos of The French
Dean Street

Toileteers waiting in the always crowded ante-room to use these popular small loos in Dean Street are offered refreshment by Gaston and his faithful staff. In the entrance room to the **Ladies** upstairs a chair – which is more than many establishments ten times this size bother to offer tired and emotional lady Toileteers. In the **Gents** downstairs, 1 small cubicle (some exciting wife-swapping invitations and numbers inscribed on the door on the day of my visit), standing room for four thin or three fat Toileteers, and a tiny basin to wash one hand in at a time.

The loos of The Curzon Cinema
Shaftesbury Avenue

There is a £5 entry fee to these loos, but the ticket does entitle you to watch the film in the adjacent premises. In fact, on this particular day, most Toileteers were ignoring the loos to do just that – it was a film in which public loos are extensively featured, *Prick Up Your Ears*, the story of Joe Orton the playwright – who had his first 'experience' in a public loo in Leicester – and from which I learnt that persons of his persuasion in England refer to public loos as Cottages, and in America as Tea-houses. I was unable to identify the London public loo in which the orgy scene took place.

However, back in the loos here. The **Ladies**, a large premise with 3 cubicles, 3 hand-basins, 3 chairs and a good dressing table, but it seemed little used. And in the **Gents**, 3 cubicles, 6 stalls (that's what it says your're paying for on your ticket, stalls), 3 hand-basins. Also the same sounds of constantly dripping water, of air-recycling machinery, and water flushing down porcelain as in a thousand such loos in London – in other words, nothing very different about the premises, and certainly no signs of any orgies taking place, having taken place, or about to take place. A pity.

The loos of The Palace Theatre ★
Cambridge Circus

Descend the staircase by the box-office and wander the ornate red-carpeted corridors which lead towards the Brasserie Bar and Restaurant and you will find them. The **Gents** a little like something out of *Les Miserables*, low-ceilinged and shaped like a coal-hole, but with 2 new loos and hand basins as well as 12 really old urinals (2 boarded up and badly in need of restoration) by that Master Urinal Maker, Emanuel of Marylebone, examples of whose porcelain masterpieces are increasingly rare.

The **Ladies**, in a vaulted basement nearby has 7 old-fashioned cubicles with heavy brass fittings, 2 hand-basins, and the room littered with various useful pieces of cast-off theatre office furniture.

The loos of The Groucho Club

45 Dean Street

Whoever designed the very smart loos down the unisex stairs here is to be congratulated. He (or she) understands what the modern Toileteer wants. A theatrical black and white motif in the tiling and hand-basins in each cubicle – which is rare, and also very sensible and face-saving in the event that you have absolutely filthy finger-nails you don't want anyone else to see you have to clean – as well as for others outside (those who pride themselves on their clean finger-nails). The loos are typical of the very chic new loos springing up in very chic new places in this area (like the ones in Moscow (the club) further up the street). The only trouble is, how do you get into them, past the good-looking and obviously efficient lady at the desk inside the entrance door if you're not a Member, or haven't come to meet a Member? 'Well I don't know his name, but he told me to meet him in the loo downstairs', – I can just see that lady believing you.

The loos of Chinatown
Gerrard Street area

There's a big shortage here, but I understand a large and decoratively Chinese one is planned for construction at the Newport Court end of the pedestrian precinct. In the meantime I would recommend, of the many loos of the many Chinese restaurants in Gerrard Street, the Loos of Loon Fung (for Reservations phone 437-5429). Go straight down to the kitchens and you will find 2 cubicles and 3 hand-basins with enormous old taps and marble tops. At least, I think they're loos. Not being over-conversant with the preparation of Chinese food and what sort of bowls and boards they use I just might be in error.

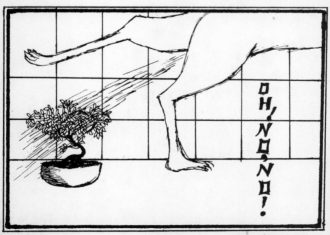

aPICELLa

THE LOOS AROUND PICCADILLY CIRCUS

The loos of The Trocadero Centre

7 Coventry Street

The loos of this great complex of cafes, shops, exhibitions, gardens, waterfalls and above all, indoor *space* – are in the French Quarter on the lower ground floor, just by the Parisian sidewalk cafes – but they are far from being seedy Parisian loos.

Entry is through one 10p turnstile, Ladies then being directed to move to the right, Gents to the left. At the same time this scene is being filmed by a closed-circuit TV camera and shown on a screen positioned above the turnstile, which, initially seems pretty pointless, because the attendants on duty in the glass box by the turnstile can see perfectly well who's going into or leaving their loos. This filming is not for their benefit, however, but for that of the security people in the operations room of the building who have cameras all over the place just to check up on Curious Happenings or Outbreaks of Rowdyism – I say 'everywhere' but I didn't

Le Coprophage
RESTAURANT
PARIS RUE DE MERDE 44 TEL.

apice

actually see any *inside* the loos. And surely no one in this country is going to be so rotten as to *hide* cameras in them?

Each loo is dominated by a sign reading: WARNING – SECURITY DETECTION SYSTEM IN OPERATION. STRICTLY NO SMOKING.

So, in the **Gents** we have 4 cubicles with ashtrays fitted on the walls beside the lavatory basins and ash in them – but a curious coloured ash. And in the **Ladies** we have 6 cubicles, each with ashtrays fitted beside the lavatory basins, not so much ash in them though. What sort of a Security Detection System is this? Were these smokers detected, and if so what happened to them?

Also in the Gents, 4 hand-basins and an incredible stainless steel trough. And in the Ladies, 5 well-lit and mirrored hand-basins. Good loos, but just slightly worrying ones.

● ● ● ● ●

At the top of this building is the permanent exhibition of the Guinness World of Records (based on entries in the famous Book). Beside the box-office is the Guinness Book-shop and quite clearly at the back of this I could see a door marked Toilets. I asked the box-office lady if my Inspector of Ladies and myself might visit them and she said only if we pay £3.20 each to visit the exhibition. This, I reckon, gets the loos of the Guinness World of Records into the Guinness Book of Records as being among the 10 most expensive loos to visit in London.

The loos of The Criterion Brasserie

Piccadilly Circus

These are adequate small loos toward the end of this historic room but, it is not, I would submit, for their fittings that you will wish to visit them. More for the splendour of the approach to them, down the great Marble Hall, its walls inlaid with rubies and semi-precious stones and its ceiling totally covered in gold mosaic making it one of the most splendid public rooms in London. (They serve a good cup of tea as well).

The loos of The Cockney Pride
Piccadilly Circus

Right through from the Piccadilly entrance, which promises Traditional Cockney Fayre within, past the bar serving Hot Grub and Cold Nosh and the loos are behind the doors marked Pearly Kings and Pearly Queens. In the **Pearly Kings**, 2 Cockney cubicles, a Cockney trough and 2 Cockney hand-basins. In the **Pearly Queens**, amid a tapestry of old pieces of printed Cockney carpet and assorted split and broken Cockney melamine floor coverings, 2 good clean loos with hand-basins and mirrors, the whole looked after by a Traditional Cockney Queen.

The loos of The Regent Palace Hotel
12 Sherwood Street, Piccadilly Circus

Through the hotel's city-of-a-foyer and down a stairway covered in one of London's dirtier carpettings to the **Gents**. Large, plain and unmemorable. The post-card offered for sale by the Hall Porter in the foyer, of the Hotel's Hairdressing Saloon (circa 1920) gives some idea of what the loos must have looked like once, and oddly, he does quite a brisk trade in these cards – curious souvenirs of their stay in London for Americans to send back to their loved ones.

The **Ladies** here are down a further flight of tatty stair-carpeting, vast enough to accommodate several coach-loads of Toileteers, and as well as everything essential, 2 green upholstered swivel chairs. Relics of the old Hairdressing Saloon? The Management had been advised that Swivelling was all the rage? Or simply a lady Toileteer who'd bought them in the neighbourhood on impulse, and then got fed up with carrying them around and dumped them here?

★ The loos of The Cafe Royal
68 Regent Street

I must say, it's the first time I've ever had a glass of champagne offered to me off a tray held by a tail-coated butler at the entrance to a Gents. I thought things must be going alright for Lord Forte if he's doing this throughout his entire chain of loos, but then it occurred to me that the Gents on the first floor here is in the Elysée Suite and perhaps sometimes when a reception is going on it may become difficult for the butler to distinguish between Toileteers and the overflow from the reception.

Inside this **Gents**, accommodations for 4 Toileteers seated, 5 standing, 3 abluting, and beside the hand-basins little bottles of – no, not more free champagne – but Sparkling Ashbourne Natural Water. Still, that's something you don't get in every loo.

Ashbourne Water also on the vanity units of the rather smart – if ungallantly positioned **Ladies**, one staircase above. 8 cubicles, 6 hand-basins in marble, a boudoir ante-room with stools, mirrors and good lighting.

In a more ornate **Ladies** on the ground floor leading to the Cocktail Bar is an elaborate centre-piece to the room like a fountain garlanded in flowers, concealing 4 hand-basins; and 4 cubicles each with, as well as a loo, a marble shelf and stool for making-up, or just sitting drinking the omni-present Ashbourne Water. This is the loo, which, despite who uses it these days, was patronised by Whistler and Oscar Wilde and all their circle. The small loo labelled **Gents** off the Cocktail Bar (1 cubicle, 2 stalls, 2 hand-basins) was part of the dining area in those days – but this needn't deter you from dropping your epigrams in it, just providing they're funny enough.

THE LOOS OF LEICESTER SQUARE

Admission to the large public loos at the top of the square is down steps which take you under the square and then through the modern equivalent of a turnstile, which only lets you in if you first placate it with a 10p piece. Very tasteful mosaic tiles (including many rare gold ones) on all the walls. In the **Gents**, 14 cubicles (some of the most graphic and decorative graffiti in town inside them), 18 stalls (including 4 for Dwarfs), a good set of hand-basins, as well as other little

basins scattered around (one of which at the time of my visit appeared to be baffling a Japanese Toileteer – he was standing beside it gargling with his trousers down – which for all I know is how any decent self-respecting Japanese Toileteer behaves in the loos of his own country). Also in the premises, a Durex Featherlite machine, and a charming attendant of West Indian origins – having great difficulty in explaining to a lady who I assumed was attached to the half-naked Japanese gent that she couldn't come into the loo even through the exit gate – which she was attempting to climb over.

This was making life very noisy for the rest of us on account that every time someone passes through this exit gate, or it is touched, something like a fire-bell rings in the place, so it was ringing quite incessantly during this little incident, and there were some very startled Toileteers looking out of their cubicles and wondering whether they should evacuate no matter how they were dressed.

Meanwhile, over in the quieter atmosphere of the **Ladies** (also 10p turnstile entry fee) my Inspector counted the contents there: 12 cubicles (including 1 for invalids and 1 for children), 3 hand-basins, a weighing machine, the normal pre-pasted toothbrush dispenser, a machine selling panty pads and tights, another dispensing Vanity Packs, and, most rare of all in any Ladies loo, a Durex Featherlite machine. Westminster Council are to be congratulated on this very sensible breakthrough – other Councils please copy.

● ● ● ● ● ●

At the bottom end of the Leicester Square pedestrian precinct are two of the new automatic 10p loos; also 2 of the new dark-glass telephone booths. Strangers to the capital are exhorted to be quite clear in their minds which is which before they attempt to make use of them.

It struck me that the new automatics look like nothing so much as plinths (or pedestals). And as Shakespeare stands on a plinth (or pedestal) in the middle of the Square, why not decorate the automatics with statues of famous Toileteers, like Thomas Crapper and Isaac Shanks. Over to you, Westminster Council.

THE LOOS OF HAYMARKET

The loos of American Express
6 Haymarket

These, once some of the finest and most sought-after loos in
London are no longer available to the public. The Security
people there said go to MacDonald's over the road which,
we found, is also where the people who queue all day to get
into Phantom of the Opera at Her Majesty's Theatre prefer
to go.

The loos of the Design Centre
28 Haymarket

There are loos here, upstairs, through a door totally – or
perhaps deliberately – unmarked. Near Umbrellas and
Luggage though. My Inspector of Ladies and I, having asked
many members of the staff for their whereabouts, having
failed to find them, having finally found them, having visited
them, were standing outside them discussing their various
contents. We were admitting ourselves a little disappointed,
not so much in their smallness but that these loos of all loos
in Britain did not contain the very best work of persons who
have designed modern loos, like Robin Levine, or Diana
Casson (whose remarkable loos are fitted in the Chartered

Society of Designers but not, alas, always available to members of the public). A very watchful male person, presumably not unconnected with the running of the Centre, approached us and asked us,'What were we doing?' I answered, feeling curiously criminal, 'Making Notes'. 'Well', said the male person, 'We don't normally like people writing about us without first having read what they've written'. 'You need have no fear of us', I responded, *we are your friends*. He looked a little startled, and we walked away, but all the same, because of his admonition to us, I won't describe here the exact contents of his loos.

● ● ● ● ● ●

It's happened every now and then, during the compiling of this Guide, that I've been looked upon with great suspicion, as I've been studying the contents of loos. In one establishment there were so many hand-basins on show that I was having to count them, in child-fashion, pointing with my finger, and every now and then write down in my notebook how many they totalled. A man who, I suppose, was something to do with the place, looked at me and asked 'What on earth are you doing?' 'I'm counting the hand-basins', I replied.'Whatever for?' he asked. 'I like counting things, *don't you?*' I replied in my best totally mad voice. He left the room rapidly without even pulling up his zip.

apicella

THE LOOS OF TRAFALGAR SQUARE

The loos of The National Gallery

Small Galleries where permanent exhibitions of 20th century wash-room furnishings are on view are situated off the basement passage (lined, claims the notice, with the works of the current Artist-in-Residence) and which leads to the Restaurant. In the **Gents** Gallery, 6 cubicles each containing a lavatory basin and cistern (but none of them containing any Artist-in-Residence), 12 stalls and 8 hand-basins – all of which place the Toileteer in some slight quandary if he has read Article No 9 of the Gallery's Regulations displayed outside. '*Visitors shall not touch any picture, frame, glass, or label* **or any other exhibit.**' In the **Ladies** Gallery, 10 cubicles each of which has 2 hooks on the back of its doors strong enough to support really heavily-framed pictures, and 9 hand-basins. The three vases of Sweet Williams beside them at the time of our Inspector's visit had been left behind, presumably, by three competitive toileteering still-life artists.

Many printed exhortations not to smoke in these Galleries, which is, also presumably, why, in keeping with the National Gallery's overall Non-Smoking policy, the cigarette machine in the passage outside the loos remains empty.

★ ★ The loos of The National Portrait Gallery

These are very civilised, situated downstairs, on either side of a carpeted lounge with 3 sofas, a telephone, free *Time Out* maps of London to take away and posters of all the other art shows on in town. The **Gents**, just beyond the massive bust of Lord Nelson which used to be in the Guard Chamber at Windsor are very smart and new, with 5 cubicles, 3 stalls and 4 hand-basins. The **Ladies** with 4 cubicles, 7 hand-basins and a very well lit area for making-up (for those about to have their portaits painted) and 3 well-upholstered chairs.

You could spend a morning comfortably here.

The loos of St. Martins In The Fields

The Crypt of this famous Church is a strange, dark, untidy place, but stranger still is to find loos in it. The **Ladies** you can't get into because the door is jammed – let's hope not with Toileteers who've been there for an age behind it. In the **Gents** there's much water on the floor, 3 stalls, 2 hand-basins without soap or towels, and 4 cubicles, 1 with no seat, 1 with no paper, 1 with no seat or paper, and 1 with a seat but not attached to the basin, and no chain or paper.

I suspect this is all temporary because there were a lot of workmen milling around, meaning playing cards and drinking tea, and one of them said he thought they were turning the place into a restaurant.

THE LOOS OF THE STRAND

The loos of The Charing Cross Hotel
Charing Cross Station

They divide Toileteers into four categories in the perfectly clean but forgetable loos downstairs here. '**Gents**' who get 3 cubicles, 5 stalls and 3 hand-basins; '**Ladies**', 3 cubicles and 2 hand-basins; '**Hairdressers**' – goodness knows what they need that the rest of us don't have; and '**Pilgrims**'. Just what could be through their door? Disposable sackcloth? Readings from the Scriptures? Information please from any Toileteer entitled to use this room. A fifth door is marked '**Sauna**' and anyone of any sex, profession or religious denomination is entitled to use the facilities in it. (But Ladies Mondays only; Gents, Tuesdays to Fridays. Sauna, £6.50, Massage £9.50, Sunbed, £5.00, Work Out (whatever that means) £3.50. Also Wax treatments for eliminating surplus hairs (Lip £2.50, Underarm £4.00, Full Leg £12.00 etc). There are other loos up the great staircase which leads to the Betjeman Carving Room, but not ones specifically for Hairdressers or Pilgrims.

The loos of The Strand Palace Hotel
372 The Strand

Very wonderful woodwork and marbling in the ground floor loos, though it looks as though someone has made off with 2 of the toilets from the **Ladies**; and the great Weighing-chair in the **Gents** is missing. This hotel might do well to update its security arrangements with the increasing cunning of klepto-maniacal Toileteers.

The loos of The Coal Hole Tavern
91 The Strand

Above-average pub loos. The **Gents** on the ground floor at the back of the great bar decorated with stuffed moose heads and pre-Raphaelite ladies has accommodation for 1 Toileteer seated, 3 standing and 1 abluting. Likewise the Gents in the basement. The **Ladies** alongside this latter has 3 marbled and carpeted cubicles each with a rare rose-coloured silk lampshade, 2 hand-basins with 4 pieces of soap, a machine which would dispense Disposable Tooth-brushes if it had any in it, and *a chair* (very rare this commodity in a pub loo. My Inspector found a lady seated in it who confided she came to sit in it every day as it was 'so peaceful for thought').

All the loos on this site were founded by Edmund Kean the eminent 19th century Toileteer and Great Tragedian in 1815.

The loos of The Savoy Hotel ★

The Strand

These are really very grand (as you might expect). From the Strand entrance straight across the lobby, down the wide staircase leading to the lounge and turn left. In the **Gents**, much space, much marbling, much attendance. The available extras may not always be on view, apart from the nail files and clothes brushes, because the attendant discovered long ago that they provided a great source of temptation to customers of some nationalities. But ask him and he will produce from a locked cupboard almost any item you might reasonably need: an emergency tie, handkerchief, button and thread, tin of shoe polish and brushes, tin of Andrews Liver Salts, bottle of Malvern water, dab of really expensive perfume.

In the **Ladies** nearby, proper dressing tables with mirrors and matching stools, tissues, powders and cotton wools; prints on the walls and plants on the floors.

Another **Ladies** near the River entrance of the hotel almost as grandly furnished, and with a sofa. And the nearby **Gents** with full-length mirrors and a mysterious tap set alone in the middle of one wall such as you might attach a garden hose-pipe to if you had a garden hose-pipe on you and your man outside to wash your car.

You could make a night out of it just visiting these loos and rewarding their attendants and yet still probably have change from a £20 note to spend at the bar.

The loos of The Waldorf Palm Court
Aldwych

The time to visit these loos is on Fridays, Saturdays and Sundays between 3.30 p.m. and 6.30 p.m. when there's Tea-Dancing going on in the splendidly old-fashioned lounge to the strains of the Modern Syncopated Orchestra. The **Gents**, on the left of the street entrance, with accommodations for 10 double-breasted Tea-dancing Toileteers standing, 3 seated, and 5 straightening their ties and centre partings over the basins. In the purple-carpeted **Ladies**, a lot of Tea-dancing ladies with back-combed hair and flowing apricot dresses, 4 wood-panelled cubicles, 4 rather glam hand-basins, 4 chairs, an armchair, and a separate large mirrored dressing-room for doing quick changes between numbers.

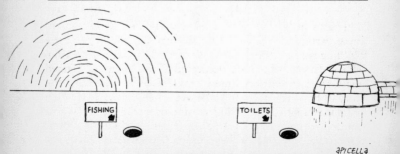

FISHING

TOILETS

APICELLA

THE LOOS OF COVENT GARDEN

The loos of St. Pauls
Covent Garden

This branch of the Westminster Council chain of public loos, virtually in the crypt of the church at the west end of the Covent Garden pedestrian precinct is one of the best-run in London. The 6 Free cubicles and basins in the **Ladies** spotlessly clean, the 20p 'Freshen-up' sachet and the 20p Disposable Tooth-brush holders both full, a nice class of younger Toileteers, many foreign-speaking, patronising the place. The **Gents** (4 free cubicles, 3 hand-basins and a long row of stainless steel cow-troughs for standing Toileteers), also has a remarkable machine (insert 1x50p and 1x10p) which delivers an Overnight Travel Pack – razor, shaving cream, aftershave lotion, shoeshine cloth, disposable toothbrush and comb (but no condom). Nevertheless a remarkable bargain these days. Also a 2x10p pre-pasted disposable toothbrush machine if that's the only part of your toilet you're interested in, and a 10p shoe polishing machine.

Opening hours of both establishments, 6.30 a.m. to 11.30 p.m.

The loos of Rules
Estbd. 1798, *Maiden Lane*

While there are some female Toileteers who complain that their new **Ladies** room on the first floor, near to the **Gents**, is too clinical and not at all what it was – the grandest privately-run loo in the capital – when it was on the ground floor. Still both loos must be counted as very civilised little oases in these parts. Indeed, their very survival on any floor of the building is one of the great sagas of modern-day toileteering. The walls of the Gents, decorated with dozens of framed pages from the establishment's old Visitors Book, tell the story of how Toileteers from all over the world rallied when there was the threat by Multi-nationals moving into Covent Garden to demolish the Loos of Rules. I quote from their testimonials on some of these pages: 'My father was a regular here – I hope my son will be able to say the same.' 'A precious piece of Old England where one finds a real welcome.' 'There is nowhere else left in London to go.' And eventually, when these pleas went with the Appeal to the House of Lords, their Lordships, voting from their seats of power, ruled against the Multi-nationals moving in and the Loos of Rules were saved for a further generation of Toileteers to appreciate.

Adjacent to these sacred Loos is the good if slightly pricey eating establishment which many Toileteers will remember was attached to the old Loos.

The loos of Joe Allen's
Exeter Street

At the back of the restaurant and turn left through an unmarked swing door into a lobby containing two yellow telephones and doors to **Gents** (1 cubicle, 2 stalls, 2 mini-basins) and **Ladies** (2 cubicles, 2 basins). Very clean but also very crowded, advance booking advisable – phone 836-0651.

The loos of The Lamb and Flag
in the little cobbled alleyway called Rose Street, off Garrick Street

Typical small pub loos, these ones especially convenient for Moss Bros or if you are not welcome at the Loos of the Garrick Club opposite. Charles Dickens was one of the famous Toileteers who patronised the Gents here so it could be that some of the graffiti on the back of the door (mostly of the 'preserve Wild Life Pickle a Squirrel' variety) was penned by him.

The loos of The Mountbatten Hotel
Monmouth Street

In fact, the loos downstairs are about the only public rooms in the almost brand-new Mountbatten Hotel at Seven Dials which do not display a dozen pictures or pieces of memorabilia of the great man – unless, indeed, it was once his shoe-cleaning machine that they have in the **Gents** (room for 2 seated, 6 standing, 4 abluting). Use of this machine is free, but dangerous I suspect – unless it has some magical way of distinguishing the colour of your shoes – or maybe I just didn't

aPICELLa

understand the instructions. Anyway it's ideal for any Toileteer wearing a brown shoe on his left foot, and a black one on his right. The nearby **Ladies** (4 smart cubicles, 4 smart hand-basins) boasts nothing like this, but there are baskets of rose petals and lavendar beside the basins, probably more appreciated there than in the Gents.

The loos of The Zanzibar

30 Great Queen Street

The 4000 word entry on these loos – not so much a vivid word-picture of their fixtures and fittings – but more about what goes on around them, why some gaggles of Toileteers spend so long in them and what they look like when (and if) they come back from them, has been deleted on the advice of our solicitors. Anyway, it's a Club, and you should be a Member to get in.

THE LOOS OF FLEET STREET

The loos of Lincoln's Inn

There are so many loos of interest in the grounds and buildings of Lincoln's Inn itself that there is a very strong argu-
ment for the setting-up of some such body as the Society for
the Preservation of Ancient Loos, and having the whole Inn
designated, and opened to the public, as an Area of Out-
standing Loos or, indeed, Lincoln's Inn National Loo Park.

However, while all Toileteers may use the pretty, ivy-
covered, ill-smelling premises run by Westminster Council in
Lincoln's Inn Fields just outside the main gate of the Inn (the
Gents of this establishment has 2 cubicles, 2 stalls, 1 hand-
basin, 8 plastic buckets of varying sizes and a rather dubious
reputation) the only loo available to visiting non-legal
Toileteers in the Inn itself is the small 4-stander off Star Yard.
The iron panels of this Grade 2 Loo, though unstamped, are
unmistakeably by Buxton of Liverpool, and the full-length
urinals late Potters. Some glass roof panes were added in the
1950s making the upper part of the premises reasonably dry
on any typical English day. It is probably easier for Gents to
use than Ladies, unless Ladies visit in threesomes and two of
them keep guard at either entrance while the other goes
within.

This loo remains open all the time on account of the fact
that it has no doors and therefore cannot be closed. (But
non-legal Toileteers will find that the gate of the Inn is closed
to them between 7 p.m. and 5 a.m.).

Other loos off Star Yard on the East side of New Square are
interesting because they proclaim the segregations that are
still practised in this ancient Inn. One set, with rather grand
fittings, is labelled MEMBERS AND TENANTS ONLY.
Another set – less grand fittings – is labelled BENCHERS
ONLY. A third set – very modest fittings indeed – is marked
ONLY FOR CLERKS EMPLOYED IN LINCOLN'S INN.
And a fourth set, the fittings of which I shall not describe to
you, is marked just LADIES.

Of the loos inside the buildings one of the more interesting
is that off the entrance to the Great Hall, designed for stand-

ing and abluting legal Toileteers only and which features a
now very rare cistern by John Bolding of Grosvenor Works.
Connoisseurs of John Bolding cisterns need to get themselves
invited to dinner in Great Hall to avail themselves of the
opportunity of appreciating this fine specimen.

The Seats of Justice (or loos of The Law Courts)

The loos of this great Gothic pile were opened by Queen
Victoria in 1883. There have been many changes since then,
the addition of loos for Ladies, of Barristers Robing Rooms,
of Judges in Chambers. The most easily found public loos
(free) are clearly signposted in ecclesiastical lettering as you
walk through the Main Hall. Clean, simple little places, the
Ladies with 2 cubicles and 2 hand-basins; the **Gents**, 2
cubicles, 2 stalls and 1 hand-basin. In one cubicle I inspected
was inscribed on the door '*Submissive woman wanted for
spanking and light whipping. The right applicant could also be
employed full-time for light household duties.*' I can just see the
set-up, but I still don't understand how the 'right applicant'
gets to see the vacancy for the position if it's advertised only
in the Gents. Or are some of the Gents who use these places
not Gents at all? Oh dear, whatever did Queen Victoria
start?

These loos are open from 7 a.m. to 6 p.m.

The loos of El Vino's

47 Fleet Street

Most of the Loos of Fleet Street have been re-sited in Wapping. Of the few which survive here I tried first the loos of El
Vino's. I enquired of a person behind the counter where in
the premises they were situated. Downstairs, he replied, but I
regret you can't use them as you're not wearing a jacket and
tie. I was in fact, the one cunningly concealed by a sweater,
the other by an overcoat, but as I had no intention of discussing the details of my dress or even undressing in this public
atmosphere, I made to leave. Then just before the door, a
customer of the establishment, a female person of my acqua-
intance – wearing very blatantly, I later recollected, a jacket

and tie, greeted me and asked what I was doing in these parts. I explained the circumstances and she said how ridiculous and to join her in a glass of wine. But alas, no, for when she ordered it from the person behind the bar he had to tell her he couldn't serve such refreshment to a Toileteer not wearing tie or jacket.

We left to sample the toilets and wines of the less dress-conscious establishment across the road.

The loo of St. Bride's Institute
Bride Lane EC4

It is a small adventure wandering into this seemingly empty almost derelict building and descending to the basement, any moment you expect to hear soft zither music and see Harry Lime emerging from the shadows. I gather the place was an ancient swimming-pool which has now been converted into a ping-pong parlour. Anyway, if you search around long enough you'll come across a cupboard with a loo in it, but its condition may make you grateful for the new automatic loo situated round the corner under Ludgate Bridge.

THE LOOS OF THE CITY OF LONDON

The loos of The Old Bailey

The Public Viewing Gallery entrance of the building leads to little loos off the staircase leading up to the Court Rooms. (**Ladies** on the 1st floor, **Gents** on the 2nd). But no camera or hold-alls are allowed in these loos and there's a man at the door to make sure you don't try to smuggle them in. However, should you be thus armed when you need to visit the place, there's an enterprising lady in the Wool Shop across the road who will look after them for you (30p your camera, 50p your hold-all).

These loos close during the lunch hour, and so toileteers in need at the time are recommended to use the ***loos of The George*** over the road — upstairs and clearly marked, 1 cubicle, 2 stalls and 2 hand-basins in the **Gents** as well as evidence that someone used an axe to try and smash down the door between these facilities. 3 cubicles and 2 hand-basins in the **Ladies** and warning notices about keeping watch on your hand-bag.

This does seem a slightly dangerous area to go toileteering.

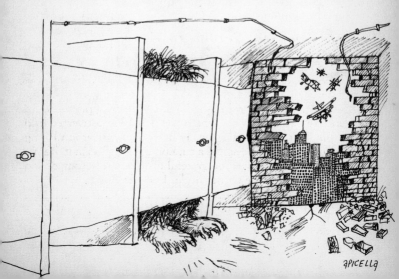

The loos of St.Paul's

These loos, not necessarily designed by Christopher Wren, are curiously situated in a row of shops (Souvenir, Women, Ice Cream, Stamps, Men) in Paternoster Square up the steps beside the Cathedral.

In the **Gents**, much brass and accommodation for 6 Toileteers seated, 10 standing and 2 abluting.

In the **Ladies** 15 free cubicles which need to be manually unlocked by the Attendant, 1 hand-basin, and further Wash and Brush-up facilities for 15p.

The loos of The Tower of London

These loos are not for Toileteers in a hurry or who have to count their pennies. Firstly, you have to join a very long queue outside to purchase a ticket entitling you to use a loo inside the Tower. Eventually, at the cash desk you are asked to hand over the sum of £4 for this privilege. A further walk and you surrender the ticket to a Beefeater at the entrance to the Tower. The hazards are ahead of you now as you search for your loo. *'Beware – Ravens Bite'* reads one sign, *'Traitors Gate'* the next, then *'Site of Scaffold'*. What possible crimes can an innocent Toileteer commit to make him eligible for punishments like these? Leave the hot tap running? Forget to do his flies up? Fail to pull the chain? But surely, beheading is a little severe. Shaking slightly, but trying to look my most innocent, I entered the **Gents** in the Brick tower (also called Block and Axe Row, built 14th century, rebuilt 19th, walls about eighteen feet thick). Anyway, 6 cubicles, 9 stalls, 4 hand-basins, and a rather untidy annexe in which a rather untidy-looking attendant sits watching a blank TV set. And I've paid £4 just for this. Then I thought, well, Richard III peed here, Henry VII peed here, Henry VIII peed here (I hope the attendant got up and stood to attention on those occasions), and now I'm peeing here. Maybe £4 is cheap for the privilege. And at least the room has a window through which you can see grass and trees and more of the Tower and some of the City of London. No one beheaded me as I left the room. No raven bit me. I walked out a free unscathed (if almost penniless) Toileteer – and the first thing I saw outside the Tower – which I hadn't noticed on my way in – was the set of loos operated by the City of London. In the **Gents**, accommodation for 8 seated Toileteers, about 14 standing, and 2 abluting. All absolutely free unless you wanted to ablute in privacy in which case the charge for a room was 15p. That's a far cry from £4 though.

My Inspector of Ladies was so incensed at being asked to produce her £4 to see the **Ladies** loos of the Tower that she stayed outside. So I can only tell you there are Ladies loos, but not what's inside them, in the Beauchamp Tower and the Cradle Tower. And of course free ones outside the Tower.

The Public loos of The Guildhall ★ ★ ★
actually situated in Guildhall Yard, off Basinghall Street, off Gresham Street

These loos are small Palaces compared to most other public ones. Once all the great City of London public loos looked like this, now here is all that survives of a past more gracious age of toileteering and even now the dreaded threat of modernisation hangs over it; there's probably at the most only two years left that you can visit these loos and get an idea of what toileteering was like in the good old days.

Notice the gleaming brass handrail that lines the steps which leads down to the premises from pavement level, the wonderful mosaic floors that craftsmen from Italy made and laid (in 1906), the walls of polished slate and marble, the great mahogany and frosted glass doors of the cubicles, the massive porcelain hand-basins (and in the Gents the towering porcelain urinals), and everywhere gleaming brass pipes and fittings. The extinct old penny fittings are still attached to the cubicle doors even though your penny is no longer needed to open them, and of especial sentimental interest to the older Toileteer is the Notice in the Ladies, actually *carved* in marble – no cheap printed jobs in those days – reading: *'Persons using the lavatory are particularly requested to see that each towel is supplied in an unbroken wrapper and to Report any Irregularity to the Town Clerk'*. That was in the days when you could have access to the Wash and Brush up Room for 3d – 3 old pennies, as opposed to 15 new pence now.

Jim McDowall, Curator of the Gents these last two years, is rightly proud of his premises, and neither he nor his counterpart in the Ladies begrudge any moment of the time taken to keep them looking so clean and pristine. He counts among his 'regular gentlemen' both Gregory Peck and Tony Richardon, as well as the many hundreds of lesser-known Toileteers who journey from all over the world making the prilgrimage to his collection of vintage fittings.

These splendid loos may be viewed weekdays 9.00 a.m. to 4.30 p.m. but are closed at weekends *'unless something special is happening in the neighbourhood.'*

The loos of The Monument

Near Monument Street

Half the roads of the City of London seem to lead to these loos situated not under the Monument but under the road at the top of Fish Street Hill and Pudding Lane where Gracechurch Street meets Eastcheap and King William Street.

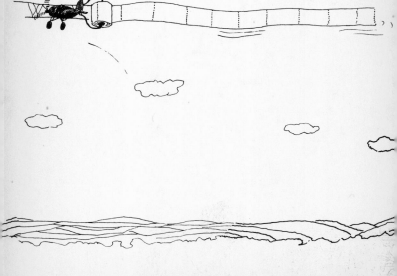

Once they were as ornate as the loos of the Guildhall but, alas, modernisation fell upon them. All that was brass is now chrome. In the **Gents**, 4 cubicles, 8 stalls (each with an ashtray above it) and 3 little hand-basins. In the **Ladies**, 4 cubicles, 2 little hand-basins.

The loos of Bank Underground Station

They are nothing extraordinary in themselves (in the **Gents** 4 free cubicles, 10 stalls and 4 basins; in the **Ladies** 10 cubicles, 5 basins) but they are built on the site of the first underground Public Loo in the world. Devised in 1855 by a Mr Jennings who, to regain his investment, made a charge to the public of one penny to use it – which was in fact the origin of the phrase 'going to spend a penny'.

The loos of The Barbican Arts Centre

We failed to find them as we could find no entry to the building on account of the fact that we couldn't find the building itself. Reports please from local Toileteers.

The loos of Liverpool Street Station

The **Gents** down some stairs opposite the entrance to Platform 5 has 6 cubicles approachable through a 5p turnstile, also 5 other cubicles marked Private. (Passengers who've held Season Tickets for over 25 years and been rewarded with a key to these? Or Porters Privies? I wasn't here long enough to discover who came to use them), 2 rows of 6 stalls curiously sited face to face in the middle of the room, 4 new recessed hand-basins, and a barber's shop with many fine old fittings. Also a 20p Durex Featherlite dispenser and a 10p weighing machine.

The **Ladies** by Platform 1, a partitioned section of the old Waiting room, is just one big mess. The Authorities feel so bad about it that they have dispensed with the 5p entry charge into the 7 broken down cubicles and are planning to open brand new loos in early 1988.

The loos of The Great Eastern Hotel

★ For **Ladies** these may certainly be preferable to the sorry quarters allotted them on the station even though it does mean walking just outside the station to reach them. These are spacious carpeted quarters, once a Writing Room, on the first floor of the hotel. Furnishings mostly in pink and pale blue include 5 cubicles, 4 hand-basins, 1 arm-chair, 1 sofa, several occasional tables and stools and masses of mirroring. Altogether a room in which you will have no qualms about dallying.

The **Gents** nearby is in the process of being totally refurbished and until that's complete you're directed to the room marked Private Staff Only. Wonderful views of the whole station through the windows above the basins.

THE LOOS OF WAPPING

The loos of The Tower Hotel
St Katherine's Dock

There are loos at the top of the stairs leading from the main entrance, but with so much renovation going on at this hotel (why? surely it only opened a couple of years ago) that they may have found somewhere else to move them to by the time you read this. They're about the only rooms in the entire building which don't have windows overlooking the river and Tower Bridge, so there would certainly be little objection from Toileteers if some of the accommodation at present allotted to mere drinkers and diners on the same floor could be converted to Toileteers' needs, and vice versa.

The **Ladies** loo on its present site has 10 cubicles, a row of 5 hand-basins and 3 good arm-chairs – almost perfect furnishing for a small bar – and piped flamenco music.

The **Gents**, all in dark blue, has 4 cubicles, 11 stalls, 10 hand-basins, an electric shoe-polishing machine and piped flamenco music. At the time of my visit, one Toileteer was in the middle of the floor demonstrating to another the steps of the tango. It might have been impromptu, on the other hand it might have been someone – the attendant? – who, unbeknownst to Management is advertising somewhere that he gives Dance Lessons here every day and gets away with it. Well, why waste good piped flamenco anyway?

The loos of The Dickens Inn
St Katherine's Dock

A lot of renovation going on here, too. The Bar loos definitely not usable at the time of writing. But there are others off the Dickens Restaurant on the floor above. In the **Gents**, 1 cubicle with 8 rolls of paper. In the **Ladies**, 3 pink cubicles with Americans in them, 1 peg, and 2 hand-basins with real flowers – yellow carnations this day – around them.

These loos, a plaque says, were opened by Cedric Charles Dickens, the writer's great-grandson, in 1976. Whether or not the persons involved in tearing them down are also relatives of Dickens there's as yet no plaque to tell us.

The loos of The Prospect of Whitby

57 Wapping Wall

What is the attraction of these old riverside loos which teem with Toileteers from all over the world and in which hardly a word of English is ever heard? To an English Toileteer there's no feature in them which makes them in the slightest bit attractive – worth a detour as it were – and yet, they're nearly always full. There's no American or Japanese who would dare go back to their homelands without boasting of having visited them. Or is it simply that they're the only loos for miles around? It's a great bafflement.

The loos of The House They Left Behind

27 Ropemakers' Fields

This pub, all alone on what appears to be a massive bomb-site – or failing that, 'Area Planned for Redevelopment', sited opposite Egerton's Agency in Narrow Street is almost unique in London in that it has not hidden its loos in an airless basement or a derelict backyard but has given over almost the whole of its very handsome first floor – once its main sitting room – to them. The food downstairs is to be recommended also. It was someone in this pub who told me that in the old days (meaning about last year), in this part of Dockland, there was no such distinction as LADIES and GENTLEMEN on the doors of loos. They simply said ABLE SEAMEN and OFFICERS.

A FEW GAY LOOS

The loos of Heaven

under the Arches, off Villiers Street, Charing X

Question: If you are wearing drag which loo do you use? Answer (at any rate in *this* establishment): It doesn't seem to matter, there's a great party going on in each. Stunningly dressed Drag Queens adjusting their make-up and wigs, fellows hard at it necking together, other fellows photographing each other wearing each others dresses. These loos, with their adjacent bars and laser-ridden dance floors teeming with hundreds of Gay Toileteers, offer some of the finest late-night entertainment in London. Open Tues–Sat. 10.00 p.m. to 3.00 a.m. Admission normally around £3.

The loos of Madame Jo-Jo's

In the **Gents** there is a perfectly ordinary cubicle, set of stalls and hand-basin, but, making use of them, femininely-garbed persons with butch voices – one actually trying to shave – and hairy legs; other young men in fur pieces, sequins, gold raincoats, whatever the visiting exotica from Rotherham are led to believe is fashionable in the capital these days. I have never seen Madame Jo-Jo himself in this Loo but he's putting on such a performance outside I doubt if he has any time to visit it. Anyway, it's another great London experience for Toileteers who enjoyed *Cage aux Folles*. Open Mon–Sat. 10 p.m. to 3 a.m. Admission around £6.

The loos of The Coleherne

261 Old Brompton Road

In the **Gents** at the back of the ground floor, accommodations for one Gay Toileteer seated, (free copies of *Capital Gay* at the doorway – but there's a perfectly adequate supply of paper in the cubicle), about 10 standing, and 2 abluting. A large blackboard on the wall for messages, or assignations or what have you (but take your own chalk), and 2 machines dispensing, I think they were called Pro-form shaped lubricated Somethings.

"For Emergency Use Only"

"For Emergency Use Only"